D1367959

Advance Praise for *Craving Grace*

"Lisa writes with energy and honesty about that mysterious, intoxicating, beautiful gift called grace—many will find themselves in her stories and experiences."

ROB BELL

"Lisa Velthouse paints a beautiful picture of her journey toward a deep, rich, and more full experience of God's grace. Her honest and witty yet profound story leads us to consider ways we may have misunderstood the very essence of God's grace and the ultimate sweetness of knowing Jesus. This book will amplify your understanding of grace."

DAVID MARTINELLI, National Director of Campus Field Ministry, Pacific Southwest Region, Campus Crusade for Christ

"Lisa Velthouse's transparency makes me laugh (and cry). But mostly, her growing grasp of grace—or it of her—challenges my mind and moves my heart to want more of the same in my life."

CONNALLY GILLIAM, author of *Revelations of a Single Woman*

a story of faith, failure,
and my search for sweetness

CRAVING GRACE

{a memoir}

lisa velthouse

SALT**RIVER**®

AN IMPRINT OF TYNDALE HOUSE PUBLISHERS INC.

Visit Tyndale's exciting Web site at www.tyndale.com.

TYNDALE, *SaltRiver*, and the SaltRiver logo are registered trademarks of Tyndale House Publishers, Inc.

Craving Grace: A Story of Faith, Failure, and My Search for Sweetness

Designed by Julie Chen

Edited by Stephanie Voiland

Published in association with WordServe Literary Agency, 10152 Knoll Circle, Highlands Ranch, CO 80130.

Library of Congress Cataloging-in-Publication Data

Velthouse, Lisa, date.
　　Craving grace : a story of faith, failure, and my search for sweetness / Lisa Velthouse.
　　　　p. cm.
　　Includes bibliographical references.
　　ISBN 978-1-4143-3577-3 (hc)
1. Velthouse, Lisa, date. 2. Grace (Theology) 3. Fasting—Religious aspects—Christianity.
4. Christian biography—United States. I. Title.
　　BR1725.V46A3 2011
　　248.4′7—dc22 [B]　　　　　　　　　　　　　　　　　　　2010048746

Printed in the United States of America

17　16　15　14　13　12　11
7　　6　　5　　4　　3　　2　　1

Author's Note

THIS IS A WORK OF NONFICTION. Stories and characters are presented here with two purposes: to portray events and encounters as I remember them and to capture the meanings that surfaced as a result. Some details have been changed to conceal identities or to simplify the story line. For instance, the character Cora is a composite. For instance, I craved chocolate countless times more than the number of occasions mentioned.

For Nathan

Contents

Introduction: After Falling   *xiii*

Part One: Two Ways to Remember
In Smallertown   *3*
The Honey Project   *13*
That Was Then   *19*
Feeling Unled   *25*
On Community and Coincidence   *31*
Take Me or Leave Me   *41*

Part Two: Withouting
Waiting on Change   *49*
God as a Vegetable   *55*
Sam James, the Wrong Guy   *61*
Halfsies   *69*
E-Flirting   *75*
Prayer by Typo   *81*
Faith Playing Fair   *85*
Tremendous and Awful News   *93*
Greenlessness   *99*

Part Three: Fig Leaf
Panties and Other Catastrophes   *105*
Gut Reactions   *113*
Smartly   *119*
Waiting: Woe Poker   *127*

Shrink   *133*

Rude, Nude   *139*

The Farm Ladies   *143*

Part Four: Cheap Sweet Counterfeit

Silent-Competitive Preaching   *149*

Switch   *153*

Not Testing the Lord   *157*

Losing Franklin   *161*

Riding on Grace   *171*

Chastity Belt   *175*

Only Brotherly   *181*

Signed Up   *189*

Sexy, Cursing, Drinking Phase   *195*

Part Five: By Flock

Strong Again Faster   *201*

Busy Household Bandit   *207*

Hide-a-Fast   *211*

In Judgment   *215*

To Ashes   *219*

Ladder Ways   *223*

Freeloading Ain't for Sissies   *227*

Fifty-Two Sundays   *235*

Acknowledgments   *237*

Notes   *241*

About the Author   *243*

"Not anything that we ever did or were, but something that was done for us by another. Not our own lives, but the life of one who died in our behalf and yet still is alive. This is our only glory and our only hope. And the sound that it makes is the sound of excitement and gladness and laughter that floats through the night air from a great banquet."

FREDERICK BUECHNER, "THE ROAD TO EMMAUS"

Mike Teavee: Why is everything here completely pointless?
Charlie Bucket: Candy doesn't have to have a point. That's why it's candy.

CHARLIE AND THE CHOCOLATE FACTORY

Introduction:
After Falling

IF YOU SPEND any time at all in churches, you're guaranteed
to hear at some point a preacher talk about the stupid-
ity of sheep. "Senseless, idiotic creatures," he'll proclaim
to the congregation, and he'll have plenty of pasture tales
to prove it. Sheep running from a photo of a wolf. Sheep,
a whole flock of them, plummeting to their deaths after
attempting to jump a fifty-foot-wide ravine. Sheep getting
blinded by sunlight because they won't move to the shade.
Sheep eating dirt. With these stories entered as evidence,
the preacher will turn to Psalm 23 and read, "The LORD is
my shepherd" with a knowing smile, and what he'll tell you
next is that the Bible is saying we're all a bunch of ignorant,
bleating failures.

A lifetime churchgoer, I've heard more than a few varia-
tions on the sheep-are-stupid metaphor, but I've never been
fully sold on it. At one time or another I've even resented
some of its spiritual implications. While I like to think I've
embraced my own laundry list of flaws and shortfalls, I
also like to view myself as at least somewhat capable and

intelligent, more a success than a flop. Put me in a pew for thirty minutes of hearing about ewes careening off the side of a mountain, and it's likely that by sermon's end I'll have tuned out the pastor.

But a few months ago I watched the director's commentary of a period film set in the English countryside. There was a flock of sheep that trotted across one of the frames, and at that point in the movie the director stopped whatever else she was saying and pointed out that filming had happened just before shearing season. The coats on the sheep had grown so thick and long, she said, that the animals would be standing one minute and the next they would've tipped over from their own weight. Crew members had to go and put them upright again.

I think it was one of the best sermons on Psalm 23 I've ever heard; it cut right through me. It brought to my mind's eye a reel of scenes and memories, moments from my former self. In those scenes I saw and recalled the person I used to be, the faith I used to lug around with me. It was a faith full of rules and behavior requirements, of To Do and Absolutely Do Not lists that had somehow seemed imperative because of Jesus. I saw my long timeline of squeaky clean living—it spanned decades and began with an impressive row of shiny stars next to my name on the Sunday school roster. I saw those stars and how much they had mattered to me, how over the years they and other accolades had become my faith trophies, won by always doing things right and right and right. I saw the structure and rigor and the matted, dirty-wool religion of it, how impossibly heavy and burdensome it had all become in the end. And I saw, too, that my knee-jerk reaction, even after everything, was to be that same dumb sheep still.

Here is where this particular story has its beginning and its end: one night a little over three years ago, at the long-past-pubescent age of twenty-four, I had my first and my second kiss. This is an odd and awkward detail to share, yes. But the odd and awkward truth is that by then I had turned a common thing, kissing, into a sort of capstone. I had built other things around and upon it, had given heft and importance to it, with good intentions and without realizing that the weight couldn't hold. Looking back, it makes sense that when my system of faith started caving in, the first big crumbles happened there. Part of the fallout now is that it is impossible to tell my story without also telling of the two kisses.

They happened at something like 3 a.m., in the early morning hours after my younger sister's wedding. They happened with a guy who barely knew me and who probably, now that I've thought about it, was hoping for more than he got. I was lying beside him on a narrow couch in the front room of the house where some groomsmen had been staying for the weekend. I had had alcohol. The two of us weren't the only people in the house, and my drink had amounted to Not Much of Nothing Strong, but still. Those bare details might seem more sordid than they actually were—had I been less naive, chances are I would've recognized what was happening soon enough to get uptight and stop things before they could become anything. Had he known me he would have been shocked things went as far as they did.

I wasn't engaged to him. That was the problem and the biggest hitch of all.

Back then I was a little over five months into a six-month fast from sweets. Back then I was a little over five years into "saving my first kiss," which was a vow I had firmly made to God at the age of nineteen-and-never-been-kissed. Back *then*, when I had first committed to that ultimatum, kissing had seemed like the biggest deal ever.

Saving my first kiss was a pair of things. It was a book, which expressed the message in capitals and italics: *Saving My First Kiss*. It was also a lowercase, plain text, everyday habit: saving my first kiss. The latter had started first; it had started as something with profound meaning between God and me.

Before the vow there was this: I had spent much of my late teens being torn up about my lack of a love life. These days it seems frivolous, remembering how fixated I was, but my reasons made perfect sense to me at the time. The only relationship of mine that had resembled romance was a stint in fifth grade that included holding hands with a boy at a roller-skating party and being publicly given a box of chocolates and a mixed tape by said boy for Valentine's Day. I had been embarrassed by the chocolates, so I broke it off with him soon afterward, though I did listen to the mixed tape sometimes when I felt like being dreamy. For ten years after that, either no more guys had been interested in me or none had dared show it. I'm still not sure which is the true history, but in the thick of it, I, being a teenager, assumed the former.

On the scale of teenage disappointments, for me this was as bad as it could get. I felt cast aside and ugly and

clearly unwanted by every guy in the universe; the weight
of this increased exponentially whenever I reminded myself
that *also* I had never been kissed. Still, I was confident
things could turn out justly: I told myself that one moment
of romance, one single kiss, would disprove even my most
negative self-talk. Then I would know I was wantable, at
least enough to break the streak. Enough to be kissed once,
in any case.

My assumption was that God knew about my angst and
waiting. My assumption was also that in a world of liver
cancer and human trafficking and extreme poverty and
AIDS, there was no use yowling to him about first kisses.
Still, on the weakest of days, I broke form and moped
a little—silently, prayerfully, as un-annoyingly as possible, promising God I would be obedient forever if only
he would choose to come through for me on romance.
This request didn't seem like a tall order. I wasn't asking
for the whole gambit of committed love and lasting bliss;
I would've been mostly overjoyed by a fling. Yet week
after month after year, even that kept not coming true.
Eventually I came to a point where I couldn't understand
one bit of why God was withholding entirely from me,
especially considering I had always worked so hard to give
him what he asked for.

Then one afternoon in the hallway of my college dorm,
a shift happened. I was walking to my room with a mug of
hot chocolate when an idea hit me like a bolt: aside from
the whole datelessness thing, I liked my life, and I was glad
about the person I was becoming. And the thing that had
been most instrumental in God's shaping of my life was
this reality that, the fifth grade aside, I had always been

single. In the midst of my long-standing complaints, there were reasons to be grateful.

That was what led to the vow. With gratitude I promised God that until I became engaged (*fingers crossed*, I thought), I would deny myself, willingly, the first kiss I had been wanting so much. This was an offering of sorts, a sacrifice, and it felt like one. I had heard of Christians who purposely didn't kiss until marriage or engagement; my first assumption about them was that they were hyper-religious and probably strange. I wasn't ecstatic about being counted among their number. Along with that, I wasn't completely sure it was a great idea for me to pen up physical affection any longer than it had been already. Still, I guessed that the vow would efficiently limit my chances of ending up tangled in the sheets of premarital sex, which was strictly prohibited. And maybe if I made the vow, God would be happy with my extra effort. The tally card went like this: *Pros: more sacrifice; more support for virginity. Con: less making out.* The pros had the advantage, and I jumped entirely in. For a while that was the extent of it.

Then the publishing happened, and saving my first kiss became not just my life but also something of its own, with a title—capital letters, italic slant, Library of Congress number. Apart from the embarrassment it caused by directly and publicly associating me with my vow, *Saving My First Kiss* seemed a mostly good thing. It let the pain of my life flip on itself; it allowed me to talk about God's love with other young women who for a haze of loneliness and insecurity could hardly see him. There was fulfillment in that for me. As a bonus, the book also gave me opportunities to travel and meet interesting people, it became a

potential building block for a career in writing, it afforded
me a tiny dose of fame, and it provided a decently depend-
able boost to my income. Pro, pro, pro, pro, pro.

As more time passed, saving my first kiss extended further, into all the big categories that seemed to define who
I was. It helped direct how I thought about my career (a
writer), how I ordered my schedule (weekends clear to
speak at youth events), how I viewed myself (*Never been
kissed, but it's okay*), how I interacted with men (*This man
will not kiss me*), how I related to God, how I related to
anyone. Soon saving my first kiss was my most tangible
expression of my love and commitment to God. This made
sense, I thought: my vow was the fruit of a powerful experience in faith and belief. It was a vital thread woven through
every part of my life, and I was standing on stages asking
unsuspecting teenage girls to take it seriously. In that sense
I had even accepted the mantle of a role model, because for
half a decade I had been taking it seriously too.

In all that time since the vow's beginning, though, not
once had I been extended a bona fide invitation to break
it. Not until the night of the wedding, the groomsman,
the narrow couch. The day that had led up to that night
had been wonderful in peculiar ways; I was surrounded
by people I loved, I felt beautiful and full, I laughed for
hours, and more than one of the men in the general vicinity seemed to notice me and to actually enjoy my company.
It was all so wonderful it seems I forgot to concentrate.
Hours later, with him there, I was no longer saving but
having my first kiss and my second, too. Immediately
afterward the only details that seemed to matter were: he is

a near-stranger, we are lying down, there is alcohol in my system, there is no ring.

During the days and weeks that followed, I struggled to figure out whether I could let myself remember it as something spine-tinglingly passionate or whether it had been downright seedy. It seemed to be both. It seemed to be neither. Either way, it had been unanticipated and earth-shattering. I had broken my vow to God, and cheaply. Parts of everything that mattered most to me—my faith and history; my word, work, commitment, and reputation—had been brought into question and made to seem a fraud, all because of what amounted to a perfectly cheap cliché: a few lost moments after a wedding, on a couch with an almost entirely unknown guy.

Tom was his name. These days I have to think hard for a while to remember it.

Looking back on that night now, I see it as the turning point, the moment when a cosmic alarm started going off. It rang like a jolt, forcing me to start waking up to the fact that things had been changing for a long time. I opened my eyes and saw that my world had been turned on its head— it was almost as if the light on everything shone differently. All at once, parts of life seemed more brilliant than ever. Other parts had become newly mottled and shadowy. Even the light itself was surprising. It fell in places and in ways that I wouldn't have known to predict.

For a little perspective: we are talking about just two measly kisses. In most sane lives, something like this wouldn't have stirred up a transformation. But this was my life, and it did, because to me this was failure. It was big failure: pulling a central thread and leaving everything else to unravel. My best evidence of faithfulness and devotion was no longer valid, and as the days and weeks and months went on, things did unravel. Things shredded at the edges. For a while I felt my whole system of faith was falling apart and fraying everywhere.

At the same time, it was then (when I would've least expected it) and it was there (where I felt most flawed and unworthy and lacking before God) that God proved to be true and real. Two measly kisses: they uncovered that I was incapable of earning my way religiously, that I couldn't achieve or even want goodness, that my heart at its core was sinister and dark and confused. They opened up a chance for me to fail myself and to fail God big, and thus they put me face-to-face with the gospel of grace—a grace that up till then I had never known or experienced. For the first time, I saw and tasted God's love in its lavishness. The love happened in measures that were spellbinding.

The other day I stopped into a favorite shop in my hometown. It was early and I was the only customer there, and while I browsed, the store owner asked me pleasant questions from behind the counter. Was I looking for anything in particular? she wanted to know. Did I think it might rain later in the day? Was I from the area? Which school did I go to? Did I know so-and-so, whose kids went there too? Then she asked me about my work. When I told her I was a writer, she asked what kinds of things I wrote, and I told her my current project is a memoir about grace. At this her face warmed up and softened all at once, and she said a breathless little "Oh!" as if she had just heard maybe the best thing anybody could hear.

"That's wonderful!" she said. "Lord knows I've needed

plenty of grace in my life. And isn't it amazing," she went on, "that after you see it once, you start to see it everywhere. You wonder how in the world you could've missed it." The woman shook her head, smiling broadly.

Yes, I thought. *Yes.*

The turning point began with two kisses on a couch, but in most senses that night with the groomsman was just a venue. It was just a setup for one grace-moment in a long succession of many. There were plenty before it and there would be plenty to follow, but the kiss fallout cracked the shell and made me notice.

Had I been paying better attention during the months that led up to the incident, in particular during a long period of fasting from sweets, I might've noticed that there had already been, over and over, decadent displays of God's grace. There had easily been enough to knock out my bland expectations. His grace to me had been conspicuous and clear, strung like a banner across the sky. When I began paying attention, it changed the way I looked at everything. I started to see grace everywhere.

But before that could happen, first there was the unraveling. Before daylight broke on the morning after my sister's wedding, in the long hours that followed my first kiss and my second, I lay on a couch, wide awake and thinking at full tilt. Tom the Groomsman was still beside me, and I was avoiding physical contact with him as much as possible, folding up one of my arms between us and carefully keeping my feet pointed toward the ceiling.

Not half a day earlier I had let him touch my face with his fingertips, and I had let everything within me whirl around that single point of contact. It had felt like a quiet, brash understanding between the two of us, something like purpose and permission and an enticing fire. There had been the glint of a threat in it too, which was the lure of where it might lead, like shadows closing in on promises I had made. But right then and right there I had been wanted, at least a little bit wanted, by that man. It had been the most unmistakable thrill. It had been dangerously, fiercely dazzling. It had seemed real and very bad and very good.

In the morning he snored loudly, and my brain rapid-fired to the point where I could hardly think to breathe. *Think. To. Breathe.* Later I went home and tried to fall asleep but couldn't. I tried to stop remembering but couldn't. I tried to stop thinking about kissing and couldn't. I tried to figure out how I had ended up where I was. I tried to figure out how the life and faith I had been building could keep moving forward after what had happened the night before. I couldn't.

This is the story of a sheep—of my heavy-wool religion worn for decades, a coat of belief that needed a trim. It is the story of how spiritual discipline can outgrow and topple a person, how goodness can be proved a failure. But it is also the story of a God who does not relish handing out trophies and spankings, who acts and speaks in a way that is tangibly and sweetly surprising. It is the story of a love unasked for, an explosive beauty that stoops to put things back on their feet. This is the only story I know, and it's about the miracle and magic of both needing a Shepherd and having him.

As it turns out, I can breathe more deeply after falling.

Part One

TWO WAYS TO REMEMBER

The practice of fasting, defined simply, has two components: something given up and something gained. These two happen together, but they happen in different realms. The giving up is a physical reality; the gaining is spiritual. This is a sweet mystery.

In Smallertown

AMONG THE SOCIETY that gathers in Smallertown, Michigan, it is somewhat freakish to be a single, twenty-something female who dreams of having a killer résumé and great shoes. For that matter, in Smallertown it is somewhat freakish to be a single, twentysomething female, period. Most women in their twenties here are married housewives making room for babies. "Such a great place to raise a family," is what they say, climbing into their minivans.

Two years of living in this town has made me all too familiar with its tedious particulars. Five traffic lights. Home to Pumpkinfest. Alcohol sales prohibited on Sundays. Sometimes smells like cornfield fertilizer on hot, windy summer afternoons. Suffice it to say, the place is not teeming with young professionals. But on a map, the distance between a pin for Smallertown and a pin for where I grew up represents just fifteen miles, and apparently hometown love is not only blind, it is also dulled to the stench of freshly sprayed manure. When I was offered a job here, I thought cozy thoughts about my childhood and about my parents and siblings who were living nearby, and I took it. That's how I came to have an ongoing lease, including closet space for my supply of great heels, in Smallertown. My apartment is halfway between the second traffic light and the third, in the upstairs of an old house on a street filled with toddlers and their doting, twentysomething parents.

"Oh," was what Urban Cole said when I told him where I live. Those eyes of his, that distracted tousle he put in his hair, the wry smile, the tattoo peeking out from one edge of his collar. "Oh." It dropped from his mouth with a thud. I had to remind myself then, several times, that the rent is cheap, the windows and ceilings are tall, and I have a minuscule drive to both family and work. I had to remind myself, firmly, that it can't make any difference if Urban Cole and all his charming urban friends insist on living less than a mile from a city center. Upgrading to their bigger, sleeker, beloved metro wouldn't be practical for me, let alone manageable; the commuting costs alone would be enough to bury me. My life is here, like it or not.

In other words, or not.

12:04 a.m. Awake and watching the ceiling. He already knew too many details when we met. "The one who wrote the kissing book?" was how he asked it, and I felt my eyelids spring open wider, a surge of heat spreading across my face. The question made me feel ridiculous, and no doubt a visible, blotchy pink climbed as high as my temples. Still, there was something bold about UC's asking, an odd reassurance, and I found myself returning his gaze and matching his grin like it was some kind of challenge. This was a novel twist on the familiar humiliation. He asked with a lilt in his voice that made me feel—who'd have thought?—interesting. *Hello, hero.*

He was the one who kept our first email conversation going for days, and he was the one who initially turned things personal. Those eyes, that smile! We talked literature, discussed weekend plans. He complimented my insight, singled me out in a crowd, arranged to introduce me to his married female friend. And did he just steal a glance at me from across the room? Did something spark in the air between us? I swear he did. Of course it did. The lilt explained everything. So three weeks ago, Thursday at 9:54 a.m., I sent the calculated but oh-very-casual email. UC, you and I should go out for coffee sometime, was the gist of it. What could that hurt? By 8:42 a.m. of A Day Later, his silence was already so weighted it was turning me panicked, obsessed, pathetic. The next time we saw each other, he was awkwardly kind, and when he spoke to me he twisted up his face a little, which I understood to be an attempt at apology. I went home, thought about the lilt again, and cried like a preteen. It was roulette for the self-esteem, that lilt.

12:16 a.m. Wondering what the rest of the tattoo looks like. Yesterday he made eye contact but stayed distant. I've been scratched off the list, that much is obvious. Too eager—gentlemen, warn all your friends. How could I have missed seeing the gaps and the contradictions?

12:19 a.m. Regretting, sighing. The lamp beside my bed is casting an orange glow into the high corners of the room. The lampshade is crooked and its base is all wrong, and that color is ugly; I obviously shouldn't have bought it. But there's no sense rethinking the decision now, a state away and with weeks or months of dust piled on. If I had the chance to go back and do things differently, who knows how far back I'd have to go in order for this moment to seem right.

12:36 a.m. Stalemate. It is the early hours of February 2. Which means yesterday was supposed to be the start of my third month of fasting from sweets, which was supposed to be the next step on my spiritual journey and maybe also a distraction from other disappointments—namely, the tiny-town locale, the less-than-fascinating career, the nonexistent (and this just in: delusional) dating life, the fast-approaching Summer of Weddings. It was supposed to be. But then yesterday became another day filled by regular snacking, with a final sweet downfall occurring around 11:45 p.m. in the form of an oversized fudge sundae. This has become my consistent response to fasting failure: fast even less and even less impressively. Now I'm lying here wide eyed and irritated with myself, waiting out a sugar buzz and a stomachache too.

12:44 a.m. Analyzing. (Rationalizing?) The problem is, I've been here before—if not here exactly, then someplace similar enough. Yes, certainly someplace similar enough. I've felt those moments when God stirs the soul; it is breathtaking. But perhaps five years down the line that ride has become a path followed, a story told, a book published. It was a beautiful experience, a gift, but even now I shrink away from conversations about it. I avoid storing copies on shelves within reach, because I'm older now and because printed right there on the spine is *Saving My First Kiss*, in common English and for all the world to see.

Quite the spectacle.

I'm afraid that others will find me harebrained and ludicrous because of the thing, and I can't seem to convince myself that there's absurdity in the fear too. So in most instances when I have no choice but to mention my book, I avoid speaking the title out loud. Saving my first kiss— those four words, used collectively, express things too simply at the least. At the most they suggest the book's author is a Bible thumper who's repulsed by sex. This is how I see the situation now, and this is how I saw it at nineteen, too, which is why I sobbed, snot-nosed, upon being told my first book's title had been decided. I was young and emotional then, and very concerned about what others might think. Had I known anything about publishing, I'd have called my editor immediately to tell her that I had just used up all my Kleenex and that I despised the title. But I was green and accommodating, so I went along with things. Besides, the title and the story were both true, no matter how they got spelled out on the cover.

I had never been asked on a date and had never been kissed. As far as I could tell, it was a condition not much better than leprosy or the plague. But God had stirred the soul. He had. That was the only way to make sense of this next part: I vowed to wait even longer, by choice this time, for my first kiss. I even made a little game of it, buying a supply of balloons and streamers and party hats in advance so I could celebrate when the moment finally happened. The party theme wasn't meant to be a gimmick, but I had to admit, it turned into a decent subplot and no doubt helped sell my first manuscript.

It wasn't uncommon, at the smallish Christian college I was attending then, for people to get engaged at twenty, so this vow of mine, to save my first kiss until I got engaged, didn't seem entirely unreasonable. What's another year or so when it's already been almost two decades? Most people over the age of twelve looked at me as if to say, *You were absurdly sentimental to decide this, and hopelessly naive.* I was, of course, and maybe to a degree I even knew it. But all that was beside the point because God had stirred. I had adjusted my sails to follow. Part of what made it real and true was that his presence could bring meaning out of the nonsense.

I graduated from college. I got a job. I worked for a year; I got a different job. I moved back to Michigan; I worked for another year. This was when the math stopped adding up. In the span of less than four months, my younger sister got engaged, then my older brother. My younger brother enlisted in the military, hinting that the third proposal would soon follow. All three of my siblings made plans to move away immediately after marriage: warmer climates, new jobs, new homes, new lives.

I was already up to my eyeballs in other people's love stories, career paths, and gift registries—the runt sister in her bridesmaid dresses—when my own parents, who love me, during three different family dinners prayed aloud for their children and future in-laws, and forgot to even include my name. *Lord, bless Noah and Paige as they get married and move and start new jobs in South Carolina. Lord, bless Sarah and Eric as they get married and move and look for jobs in Kentucky. Lord, bless David and Christi as they get married and move and begin their life together on a Marine base somewhere. Et cetera, et cetera, six out of seven, amen.*

The first time it happened, the irony of the oversight was almost laughable. The second time it was decidedly not funny. The third time I blinked down toward the plate in front of me, jaw agape, half inclined to throw a royal fit the minute somebody might ask me to pass the potatoes. Dinner began and ended, though, and I never said anything about it. I just sat there, smiling so as not to ruin people's appetites, listening from the fringes and wondering how and when I had come to disappear. *Lord, bless Lisa; there's nothing worth mentioning.*

My life is not awful. I remind myself of this sometimes: not awful. But it isn't what I would have expected, and compared to what I want, it seems hollow and stale. The people around me are moving onward and upward effortlessly—by contrast, the combined total of my own efforts is a slumping disappointment. Once upon a time I thought I was headed somewhere significant. Now I am twenty-four years old and living in the land of, yes, a gourd-headed scarecrow festival. I've been on two dates in my lifetime, both blind, both forgettable. I keep spending more money than my paychecks will cover, and the wedding gifts can be blamed for only a fraction of it. My job as a ghostwriter, it turns out, is best suited for someone unlike me, someone content to live a quiet life. Quiet is quite possibly the last thing I could want. Plus now I've fouled up any chances of ever glimpsing the second half of that tattoo.

The richest pieces—my family, my friends, my church community, the high school ministry I get to volunteer with, the teen seminars I'm invited to speak at every now and then—I'm not sure when they stopped being enough. What I know is that there's a surety that's missing, and the balance is off. I'm tired of being the person I've become, and it's a grueling tiredness that's been going on for so long I'm almost bored with it. How can that make any sense?

There are people who want a quiet life, sure. And people who wouldn't mind being the eternal poster child for Saving My First Kiss. Me, I'd like to meet somebody tall and spectacular, who'll place a hand at the small of my back and make me laugh until my sides cramp, who'll eventually become my reason for buying seriously scandalous lingerie. And I'd like to be part of something bigger than me—not necessarily huge, but something that halts people enough to change them. Right now I am as far away from all that as I could be. I am here. And this room around me is tinged with the light of second thoughts, orange after midnight. I am lying here thinking about God and about how I am disappointed in him, and I am wondering if I will ever feel differently about that.

And yet.

There is a jar of honey taking up space on my kitchen table. I put it there eighteen hours ago, at the beginning of fasting attempt number three, because against a glare of doubt and disillusionment, I still can't shake the idea that what I lack most in life is real sweetness. I'm hoping it's true that there is a way to experience it, discover it, and savor it. I get the sense that things might be better if I could learn how to crave it. I have a gnawing suspicion that I won't be able to move forward, spiritually speaking, until I give this fasting experiment my best shot. The soul is stirring. My stomach churns.

Stretching toward the lamp, I turn the switch and let the room around me fold into darkness. Honey will become my starting point, a fourth and final time. Six months without sweets, I tell myself, and for long moments afterward I lie awake, wondering if I'll be able to make it all the way to August. I am questioning if I'll learn anything in the process, if this will be strictly discipline or if maybe something else will break through. I am asking myself if God really could be sweet, and whether or not that would be enough to help me crawl out of this bland and frantic place I've fallen into.

The Honey Project

Sh'ma Yis'ra'eil
Hear, O Israel
Adonai Eloheinu, Adonai echad.
The Lord is your God, the Lord alone.
V'ahav'ta eit Adonai Elohekha
Love the Lord your God
b'khol l'vav'kha,
with all your heart,
uv'khol naf'sh'kha,
with all your soul,
uv'khol m'odekha.
with all your might.

I'd be lying if I said UC wasn't part of my reason for having been at the seminar in the first place. Ray began his teaching as he always does, by asking the audience to follow along in reciting the *Sh'ma*, Deuteronomy 6:4-5, both in Hebrew and in English. My mouth formed the words in response, but as I spoke, my eyes were darting from doorway to doorway at the back of the room, scanning the faces of stragglers for that familiar wry smile. Ray had long been one of my favorite Bible scholars, but when I found out UC was a fan too, it was plenty of incentive to get me to the seminar.

Miles away from the topic for the first twenty minutes or so, I finally made myself give up on craning my neck around and just accept the fact that UC wasn't going to show. By that time Ray had barreled through his introduction on Christianity's Jewish roots, and he was talking about frog study, which seemed an unlikely yet endearing reference point.

"If we want to learn about a frog," Ray said, "as Westerners our first step is abstraction: we take the frog out of the pond." He was speaking figuratively, highlighting differences between Eastern and Western thought. The scope of his metaphor held Westerners as the scientists, Easterners as poets. God, not disrespectfully, was the frog.

As usual, Ray was bounding around onstage, bursting with animation like a second grader who's just discovered there's a rocket ship in the basement. At times he got so excited that he spoke in a staccato rhythm, as if there were exclamation points scattered throughout his sentences. "We *abstract* a subject! In order to know it!" he told us. He went on to describe how Western study occurs in settings of isolation: sterile room, fluorescent lights, surgical gloves. We cart the amphibian back to Bio 101, he said, so we can identify its features and define its function. As a result, even some of our best observations have a clinical, detached quality. Their descriptions lack a reference point. *God is love*, we say. *God is omnipotent. God is awesome.* These are profoundly meaningful words, Ray pointed out, but with an airy vastness to them—not a concrete image in sight. The danger is that the frog has been dunked in a bucket of formaldehyde, stretched out and pinned to a pan, dissected and labeled by pieces. *Mighty* here. *Mysterious* there. *Fearsome* just left of the scalpel.

Instead of abstracting their subject, I learned that evening, Easterners abstract themselves. They go to the pond and watch as the frog reaches out to pull himself through the water. They train their ears to hear his croaks and burps. They get to know the feel of cattails and lily pads until the scent of the air nearby becomes familiar. They tell stories about the frog around their water coolers; sometimes they joke unmercifully about his latest girlfriend. Tangibly they discover their subject, and tangibly they express it—the frog—by way of stories and the senses.

During the heyday of the Roman Empire, about the time of the early Christian church, a strong arm of Western culture invaded the land of Israel and its surrounding areas. As a result, some writings of the New Testament display abstract, systematic expressions of theology: God is love, for example; God shows wrath; God comforts. This represents a shift, or at least the beginning of a shift, away from the Eastern mind-set of the Hebrew Scriptures (also known as the Old Testament), where God is described with figurative language throughout the text. He is a shield, a rock, a king on a throne, a hiding place. While in a way more simplistic, this Eastern view of God holds a different richness because it is palpable.

God is love has limits in the sense that it doesn't draw a better picture of God than the one I already have. There's no fixed substance to point to, because love is a feeling, an attachment. An abstract. For the record, I'm almost as confused about love as I am about God—linking the two hardly brings added clarity. On the other hand, if God is a fortress, a strong wind, a light, then I can be somewhat less in the dark about him. I've seen the Tower of London, after all, and the Stars and Stripes flying over Fort Sumter. I've heard wind whistling in the eaves outside my bedroom window, and I've known what it is to stand in the middle of a pitch-black night. God, by way of the senses. It expands him, taking him beyond the elusive confines of my thoughts and emotions, making him the deity I can feel on my cheeks, the Lord I can hear through the trees, even the God I can taste.

Back to honey, which is and was the point.

Ray told us the story of a morning he spent in a Jewish classroom on the first day of school. It was the first year of school for this particular class of kids, and at the beginning of the morning, the rabbi stood before his students with a stack of brand-spanking-new copies of the Torah, the first five books of both the Jewish and the Christian Scriptures. From that moment, the words in those books would be the axis on which all their studies would turn. Everything else to be learned or known would be secondary, would bow to this. They'd learn the Hebrew language on the pages, memorize large portions by heart, and orient their lives based on what it said. The rabbi placed a copy of the Torah on each of his pupils' desks, and the five-year-olds scooted forward, amazed at the gifts. Next the kids watched with awe as their teacher positioned a small square of waxed paper on the cover of each book. Then, from somewhere at the front of the room, he produced a palm-sized, bear-shaped plastic mold. Honey. Walking around the room once more, he squeezed a single sugary globule onto every waxed square.

The lesson that morning could have centered on study and memorization; on culture and religion; on yarmulkes and long, curly sideburns; on menorahs instead of Christmas trees. It could have referenced the stories of Abraham, Isaac, and Jacob, about how God had made them into a nation and had rescued them out of desert wandering to call them to him. It could have been about how God had promised a sacrifice in blood, about how the author of life had appeared to their people throughout history, wrapping himself up in a pillar of fire, a cloud in the sky, a voice in the bush, consuming flames from heaven. The options for an impressive introduction to Jewish school were endless. What the rabbi chose was honey drops.

He told his classroom full of five-year-olds to stick out their pinkies. They did.

"Dip your finger in the honey!" he said. "And bring it to your lips!"

The roomful of excited kindergarteners sampled sweet, sticky honey. Then there was a long, expectant pause as they waited for their rabbi to speak. When he did, it was with a voice that boomed along the walls and echoed across the ceiling.

"Never! Forget! What God! Tastes Like!"

Had I been looking for conspiracies, I might have thought honey was breeding in the days that followed Ray's seminar. Suddenly it was everywhere I went, blatantly and in unreasonable supply. Drizzled over cornbread at a friend's house. Served alongside chicken fingers at dinner one night. Stored in plastic packets in the fridge at work. Standing (previously overlooked) next to the parsley leaves in my kitchen spice cupboard. When a cousin of mine off-handedly mentioned he'd taken up beekeeping in his back-yard, I took that as the final hint.

A fast was the only idea that came to mind, and I'm still not sure why, other than that maybe I was looking for a peg to hang some meaning on. I'd fasted once before: no chocolate during Lent my senior year of high school. If I closed my eyes, I could still see the fudge-frosted, raspberry-topped devil's food cake I had to turn down at prom because of it. Torturous. Yet there was something distinct about the focus I'd felt during that season. It had been a rudder of clarity, something tangible to go back to in the times when I felt most in need of good steering. And there was no question: three winters ago I was hopelessly adrift.

Six months was the benchmark I picked for my fast, because it seemed a respectable stretch and because under the circumstances I seemed unlikely to pull myself together any sooner. Besides, that would take me through most of summer, and if things went well, maybe I could lose half an inch or so in time for wedding season.

That Was Then

THE CURRENT WINTER

My friend Drew lived and worked in the Middle East
for a while last year, and part of his time there overlapped
Ramadan. Ramadan is the Islamic lunar month of fasting:
during its twenty-eight, twenty-nine, or thirty days each
year, practicing Muslims fast from food, drink, sex, and
smoking, along with a number of other things that might
seem indulgent or excessive, every day from sunup to dusk.

Many of Drew's coworkers were practicing Muslims,
and in Ramadan they fasted. They stopped having snacks
during work hours. They stopped breaking for lunch. They
got thirsty. They got hot and bothered, probably. They had
nicotine-withdrawal fits. They talked about how much they
couldn't wait for the daylight to be gone. But they held on

until, far away over the desert horizon, the last sliver of sun went down.

During Ramadan, Drew saw quickly that fasting is the rule rather than an exception in that part of the world. Though he, a Christian, had fasted before, being surrounded by the fasts of Ramadan gave the discipline a fresh appeal. He was inspired again by its difficulties and its cravings. He respected more and more the flinty dedication it required. He even started his own lunchtime fast as a result.

Later Drew and I had a conversation about fasting, in particular about fasting from food. While we talked, he made an interesting observation about the cravings that come with fasting. He compared them to the cravings that come with dieting and with starvation. In simplest terms, he noted, all three are about having less to eat, but the hunger pangs that come from a fast have something that sets them apart. These cravings are different because they have added meaning. There could be three people—one who is cutting carbs, one who lives in an area hit hard by famine, and another who is fasting. While they might all crave the same particular something, the faster's craving would carry infinitely more weight.

There's no stoicism in fasting when the fasting is true, Drew said. There's no absence of meaning, no staleness of heart. "With a fast," he said, "the physical longing points to something that's realer still."

The physical longing points to something that's realer still. This sounded genius at the time. I even dug in my purse for a scrap of paper so I could write it down and remember it verbatim. After a few days, though, I thought more about this observation of his. I thought, too, about what the experience of fasting had been for me. And I realized that when Drew made his genius comment about meaning and longing and significance, I had just fed my stomach a pair of peanut butter cups. Getting wrapped up in the romance of the idea had been easy. Had he tried to share his thought with me three years ago in the middle of the Honey Project, back when fasting was twenty parts blood-sugar battle for every single part romance, it's possible my response might've been mildly murderous.

There are two ways to remember a fast. One is the silver-lining summary, the version people like to hear when the fast is over, after you've had some time to scarf down dessert and regroup. The Honey Project came with plenty of moments that are now memories befitting this angle. They are neat and straightforward and a little bit perky.

The second way to remember is to stay mindful of the vividness of the hunger. With this kind of remembering, it's almost as if the flavor of the fast still lingers on the tongue; it can be alarmingly un-chipper. This kind of remembering knows that in fasting, the only thing that rivals the screams of a physical craving is the megaphone shriek of the "realer still."

During the Honey Project, there were more moments of the second sort than I could try to count. They were loud enough to focus my attention immediately, ordering any competing voices into total silence. To me, these moments were God's clear voice, captivating and melodic and rich. They had me spellbound—I am spellbound still—but the hard truth about them is that most times they sounded at close range, at full shrill. Almost three years later, my ears haven't stopped ringing.

What I know now is that an experience of fasting can concentrate like a searchlight, zeroing in on a person and pointing out every shadowy form, every movement that is suspect. I know that a fast is a germinating seed; it's able to grow strong, sinewy roots that spread out and take hold and then rummage around in places where they haven't been welcomed. I know that fasting can put a choke on even the things that seem truest and rightest and most good. It can bloom into something that is truer and better, yes. And it can illuminate what is obscured or dim or seemingly far away. But first it might—it *did*—toe the line of ruining everything.

Long before the ringing and almost-ruin came into the picture, though, I found myself looking forward to Lent in a new way. I found it to be a happy coincidence that the start of the Honey Project also happened to be right around the beginning of Lent. Up till that point, Lent had been a sometimes noteworthy and sometimes neutral event in my life. I was familiar with the basics of the season— I knew that on the traditional Church calendar it was the time before Easter, set aside for remembering Jesus' forty days of fasting and temptation in the wilderness. Still, most years I hadn't observed Lent in any special way. I hadn't looked forward to it, I hadn't dreaded it. Mostly I hadn't given it thought at all.

But there I was, trying to successfully pull off a fast from my much-loved processed sugar, and just a few weeks after Day One of my being sweets free, the global Church would begin its yearly time of self-denial and reflection. I knew that as always during Lent, fasting would be The Thing. At church on Sundays, pastors would say things about what it means to hunger, to long for something but not have it. During the week there would be other fasting comrades for me to commiserate with. So I looked ahead to Lent with anticipation; I counted on its being an encouragement and a reprieve. That was then.

It is nearing three years later. It is almost Lent again, and this year I am dragging my feet about the season. My friend Kim has decided to fast from meat. My friend Tina is planning to fast from all chocolate that isn't fair trade. A guy across the hall at work claims he's going to give up sarcasm. My roommate thinks she'll give up everything that isn't a fruit or a vegetable, or maybe she'll just fast from one meal every day, Ash Wednesday to Easter. She's not sure yet. As for me, I've halfheartedly considered giving up cake or new clothes or going out to eat. Those are the things I mention when people ask me about Lent. I keep quiet about other thoughts, namely:

Every time I try to imagine a forty-day stretch without (fill in the blank), the idea alone seems like a cause for exhaustion.

I think it is actually physically tiresome to me.

This year I'm skittish about fasting. I'm suspicious about Lent and everything to do with it. I think I'm cranky, too. Obviously this is an emotional reaction, linked to more than just self-discipline and abstaining from things, and obviously I am overreacting. Probably I'm afraid of having to go through it all, all over again.

Feeling Unled

IN THE BEGINNING of the written story of God, the first
character to sweep out onto the stage is God himself.
The text is Genesis 1, and in its original Hebrew it intro-
duces God in the second and third words. *Bara Elohim.*
They announce him by his action: "God created." Next
in that first sentence are the objects of God's creating.
Et hashamayim ve'et ha'arets: the heavens and the earth.
Thus, like the most interesting of characters often do, God
shows up with great props.

The passage doesn't offer any extra details about God's
heavens, but it says God's earth was empty and didn't
have any form to it. People who read the Bible in English
know this, often by heart. We also know that at the start

of everything there was darkness upon the face of the deep and that the Spirit of God was hovering over the waters. We know this from our Genesis 1, because that's what it says explicitly in our verse 2.

Reading the same passage in Hebrew, however, we would also run across a rhyme (*tohu vavohu*) and not just one but two instances where the phrase "upon the face of" appears. These poetic elements and others didn't make the cut for our "In the beginning . . ." Students of words are not alarmed by this; it's impossible to retain every nuance of meaning in a jump from one language to another. Thus there is beauty to "lost in translation": going back to an original text means deeper digging and adds polish for our understanding. And so even more brilliant facets of the gem can be found.

I guess you could say that up till just a few years ago, I viewed God as more or less emotionally distant. Like one of those gruff, impatient men who tense up rather than shed a tear. Whose backbone stiffens whenever any-body tries to give him a hug. To me, God had always had something of a shell around him. He was the type of being who needed to be won over, who required always that I prove myself to him and earn his favor. Perhaps that's why I worked so very hard to become so very good at following his rules.

Not that I was consciously looking for evidence, but verse 2 of Genesis 1 seemed to back up my theory. It pro-vided a picture of the Lord I thought I knew: "The Spirit of God was hovering over the waters," it said. So the order went as follows: God created things (verse 1), then he hov-ered over them (verse 2). Hovered, like a hovercraft. Like a parent waiting to see that you've done your chores. Like a watchdog, a tattletale, like somebody with eyes in the back of her head. Don't screw up; he's hovering. He's as close as he can get without having to give in and touch you.

It was from this position of safe distance that God started giving commands: "Let there be light" was the first. And there was light (verse 3). This was how I viewed God. He had brought me into existence as one of his created beings, and then from far away elsewhere, he told me what to do. He expected to be pleased, and he deserved it too. What choice did I have, really, but to obey and also to find a way to be content about it? This is God we're talking about, after all.

But a little less than three years ago, while cozied up with some writings by Frederick Buechner, a skilled theologian who also happens to have been nominated for a Pulitzer, I ran across an essay that mentioned Genesis 1. In it, Buechner highlighted the Hebrew word *merachefet,* which is the one from Genesis 1 that's often translated *hovering.* Buechner said that *merachefet* is the same word Bible writers used to describe a mother bird over her nest. He said the word also means *brooding.*

I read that sentence, and I started crying all over the pages of his book. The tears rolled, and as they rolled, I thought about the months that had just passed, which were the months of my sweets fast. *Merachefet* put words and a picture to all the mesmerizing truths God had uncovered in that time. There it was, succinct and vivid: God is the mother bird, protecting and preening over and singing to and feeding. There it was: I'm the slimy, blind hatchling underneath.

What I know now—what I didn't know then—is that faith is not about my trying to close the distance between God and me by becoming better than I am, by trying to make the grade, or by working to please. It is not at all what I always thought it was—at least it doesn't begin there. Faith begins in a nest full of weak and hungry failures, unable to fly for even a moment on our own, needing the constant shelter and warmth of a strong, soft wing.

"He will cover you with his feathers," says one of the psalms.[1] This is what God taught me during six months without sweets. He taught me how to fall, how to accept that I fail and need him totally. He taught me that faith is about grace, and grace is this God who is brooding.

When the Honey Project had ended and then for a long time afterward too, *merachefet* captivated and changed my whole life. Almost any experience would make me think of God, and thinking of him would bring on a sudden, surging thrill in me. I was ravished. I knew down to my core that this was what it meant to believe. God was the God of love, full stop. I felt it. He brooded over me.

But like I said, that was three winters ago. And there is another way to remember the story.

The brooding came only after a long, hard season where I felt dragged and pulled and scraped and feeble, where I was proved to be a failure and a fraud, where everything I had always relied on fell apart. That season was painful from beginning to middle and up to the very end, and then for a long time afterward it was painful too.

Today as Lent comes nearer and nearer, my cynic's voice keeps telling me that signing on for another fast is equivalent to asking for everything to wreck and fall apart once more. This logic is on many levels unfounded, I realize, but my experience says it's not entirely baseless either. My fear is that if I were to fast again, I would have to learn again what I learned last time, and on a scale that's similar to last time too. I'm afraid that my whole world will be upturned and flipped around again, that once more I'll lose track of my bearings and myself for a long while.

Lent falls unfavorably on my emotional calendar this year. Another fast is still too hard a sell. Too much of me still feels too recently scraped raw, and I don't have the stamina to face it again.

And yet.

Earlier this month Sarah, my sister, called to say she felt led to daily pray that I would come to know the fullness of love. When I heard her say this, what I pictured in my mind were those posh and gold-toned folks of religious cable TV, the ones who say "Hosanna" and "I feel led" a lot, who are almost always either badly jeweled or perpetually beehived. Even the backdrops and stage lighting on those shows make me suspicious. So on the phone with my sister, after her "I feel led," I got instantly uncomfortable and filled the silence with a nervous giggle. But Sarah can't stand trinkets or big hair, and she's not the kind of person who goes around spouting churchy sayings just to hear herself talk.

Sarah read some verses from Ephesians 3 out loud over the phone—"that you, being rooted and grounded in love, may have strength to comprehend . . . what is the breadth and length and height and depth, and to know the love of Christ that surpasses knowledge,"² it says—and then she again used the phrase "I feel led." In that moment all the televangelist jokes that were brewing in my head dissipated, because in spite of myself the tiny hairs on the back of my neck stood up. I was sitting on a couch in an airless basement, yet it was as if I could feel that outside there had been a shift in the wind.

Since then I haven't been able to stop thinking about another fast. Or about the last one, for that matter. Or about Lent, either. It's possible I have even begun to fixate. This is a problem, because lately nothing major has gone wrong or capsized, and because what I'd like for a while is to continue the current sense of near-settledness. I'd like a couple of months where no huge flaws and faults of mine are newly uncovered, a very non-food-focused Lent where I'll eat and do whatever I please.

But every time I think about *the love of Christ that surpasses knowledge*, I feel a shiver go over my skin. I don't know what this means, but I have my guesses, and my guesses have me worried. They have me wondering whether God in his peculiar way is letting me know he has something to say again. They have me fretting about what he might say, and when and how and why, and what it might take to pick up the pieces this time.

On Community
and Coincidence

THE CURRENT WINTER

A FEW WEEKS after the phone conversation with Sarah, several things are happening in the same time period. Some of them have links of some sort, but most seem entirely unrelated.

First of the Things: I am working a lot. I have been working a lot for a long time.

A year after the Honey Project ended, I put away my ghostwriter hat on a proverbial high shelf after being offered a position as writing manager on the communications team at my church. Mars Hill is my church; it happens to be of the size that it requires a writing manager and a communications team. This position is a professional sweet spot for me—it exists to serve a community

I believe in, it surrounds me with fascinating people whom I care about and respect like crazy, it's refining skills that I'm excited to see refined, it's teaching me practices that can make me a better writer and person, and it is not— magnificent change!—in Smallertown.

I love my job. I can't imagine wanting to leave it. On the weeks when it requires forty-five or fifty hours of my time, I happily write for forty-five or fifty hours. On the weeks when it requires sixty, I happily write for sixty. Then at home I am working too.

A little over a year ago, I moved out of my Smallertown upstairs apartment and moved into a partly renovated 1970s condo with a roommate. The place is just ten minutes from a downtown metro, and our unit has red furniture, robin's-egg-blue walls, and funky black and white curtains that say, *Nobody here is looking to push a stroller anytime soon, thank you very much.* It's fantastic. In the basement, surrounded by four wood-paneled walls and a patchwork of 1970s carpet samples the previous owner glued to the floor, there is a table at which I am working to write a book manuscript.

It has been three years since the Honey Project, and I haven't been able to get that fast out of my head. For two years I have been writing about it, in little bits at a time, whenever I have spare moments. On a schedule that also needs to accommodate days at the office, laundry, cooking, grocery shopping, at least minimal time with family and friends, and an already-scaled-back volunteer gig, spare moments have been hard to come by. The more I want to write, the more ruthless I get about my protecting my schedule and paring down my commitments.

Recently I've pushed a temporary pause button on my relationships, and in my work I have ceased procrastinating. I have been writing, writing. No dinner plans, no parties, no movie nights out with the girls, no reading, no going to bed early, no wasted weekend afternoons, no walks around the neighborhood, no activities that aren't Purposeful and Productive. Maybe/probably I've gone a little overboard and excessively type A here. But the extra effort will be worth it if someday the story can be told, if a published copy of the book can one day be held in hand. That's what I've been telling myself. All it will take is more hard work.

What I need is to finish an outline of the book plus two sample chapters. That's what a literary agent would want to see before agreeing to represent me, and without an agent, chances are practically nil that a publishing house might agree to put the final product in print.

Thing with links to the First Thing: For a while now, I've been spending only a minimal amount of time in Scripture and prayer and keeping Sabbath and practicing other spiritual habits that are important to me.

Basically I read Scripture when it's required for work, I pray when groups I'm in are praying, I go to church on Sunday mornings, and that's all. For church services, I've even been sitting near the back, away from my friends, and bolting toward the door as soon as the last word is said or the last song has been sung. Reading the Bible or having to wait in the parking lot would get in the way of good writing time, I think.

Thing without links: I am getting bored with my own vanity, possibly.

Although I'm no less smitten by fashion than I was a year or two or three years ago, lately I've been thinking that I probably have more than enough clothes, that I should therefore probably quit buying more. I've been thinking it would be nice to have some accountability, some potential incrimination in this. Since there's no one sharing my bank account, and since my roommate and I are close but not in a kindly-telling-each-other-off sense, there's never anyone around to see my shoebox-sized shopping bags, lovingly turn up her nose, and say, "Really, Lis? Another pair of heels?" I think I'm wanting that. Maybe.

Thing linked to the Vanity Thing, in the sense that this is yet another Thing I should probably change about me, and linked to the Schedule Thing, in the sense that I don't take time to cook real food: I haven't been living healthfully.

It might even be a stretch to say I'm pursuing a mediocre state of health. I eat pizza at least once a week, possibly more like twice or three times, because I have a good recipe for homemade and because Domino's is close by for takeout. And with the Honey Project long since complete, I've managed to reacquire my sweet tooth. And I haven't been working out or even going for long walks. I have been writing.

Thing linked to all but the Shoe-Buying Thing: I am new to a group. Recently some acquaintances of mine, husband Kyle and wife Marie, invited me to join the Bible study they're part of.

Up till a few weeks ago, Kyle and Marie were people I didn't know well; we volunteered together in the same high school ministry, but I think in my lifetime I had had two or three brief conversations with each or both of them.

Then one day they asked me to be part of their study, telling me it meets at a house out in the country every Sunday evening. They told me that it was made up of six couples, four married and two about to be, but that the group wasn't couple-y. Such a description sounded like a complete wild card to me, especially since it was coming from a couple.

I debated what to do. From the Wednesday of Kyle and Marie's invitation to the following Sunday afternoon, I vacillated. Finally I decided that in going, there was only a chance my personality wouldn't jibe or that I would feel like the odd wheel on an evenly outfitted vehicle. Whereas in *not* going, my continued guilt about unkept Sabbaths was a sure thing. I went.

We had one of the most delicious dinners and one of the best discussions I had had in a long, long time. The people in the group were funny, hospitable, articulate, hardworking, fervent in faith, and very smart. After just one meeting, their influence and camaraderie made me want to know God better and follow him more closely. It felt like something clicked, something important that I didn't want to unclick for a while. On my drive back out of the country that first evening, I was already itching to go back. Each Sunday since, it has been the same and better.

Thing probably related to the Small Group Thing: I am experiencing nostalgia about farms.

It took just a few drives out to the Bible study before I realized I was remembering my childhood with every trip. Until I was nine I lived in farmland, with fields and a garden and a crick—not a creek, a *crick*—at the back of our family's home, with a barn off to the side that housed thousands of chickens. The memories of spring-morning *peep, peep, peep*s filling my ears are still some of the fondest I have, despite the fact that the newly hatched chicks peeping them eventually grew in size and hostility until they pecked with brutal precision at my ankles.

All these things, from the work to the shoes to the Bible study to the farm fowl, have an odd and unexpected convergence one week, about a month and a half after my first evening with the small group. Early in the week I'm sent our standard weekly group email from Kay, one of the leaders. But this time, along with the shared prayer requests and the Sunday food sign-up, there's something else, too. Kay is making certain everybody will be there the following Sunday—she says it's important that nobody misses. She says, without going into further detail, that full participation is necessary because we'll be discussing the future direction of the group.

There's no certain doom and gloom within it; still, my initial response after reading the email is a sinking in my stomach and the thought *Shoot, shoot, shoot.* I have been more excited about this group than I have been about anything in a long time. It's helping me look for God and see him, it's supplying reasons for me to cook or bake at least once a week, and it's giving me real community—people to care for and who care about me. From Sunday to Sunday, my in-box has an ongoing conversation of encouragement and updates and prayer requests and hilarious jokes and stories. The group is still new to me, yes, but its connection has been instantly strong and significant. If I had things my way, it would keep going like this for a long time.

The future of the group occupies my thoughts for

the remainder of the week, and in that time, I manage to decide one thing.

Thing: Of the six couples I've come to know through this group, there are three I already can't imagine letting out of my life.

Kyle and Marie, Kay and Matthew, and Jenny and Joe are all in one way or another on a wavelength that feels like home to me. They're inspiring, challenging, and kind—I'd like to think these are the sort of people who could support and strengthen me, and maybe for whom I could do a little of the same. That's the only piece I can be sure of as we head toward the group's future. So during the week I find myself praying what feels like a bold prayer. I think of the K&M couples and of the J couple, and I ask God to make it possible for me to keep knowing them.

That Sunday after dinner together, all thirteen of our group members begin perching in a circle around a coffee table in Kay and Matthew's living room. I wait with expectancy as we get ourselves settled, then I wait and try to pray along with the opening prayer. Then Kay starts in with a story.

She tells us that a few weeks ago Kyle and Matthew met for coffee and talked about the group, about what things were beneficial and good about it as well as what was lacking. She says they discussed the conversations we had been having about God's calling on each of our lives, that they brainstormed ways to pursue those callings more tenaciously. She tells us they discussed the geographical distance separating the group members' homes, how it limited our growth as a group. There was interest and desire to be invested in each other's lives—actually and physically

invested and involved, not just by email—more often than
once weekly. But how could that happen?

She tells us that initial coffee meeting turned into first
a lot of prayer and then another meeting. At the second
meeting, Kyle and Marie and Kay and Matthew discussed
the ways in which God might already be leading them to
change. What was discussed, she said, was that Kyle and
Marie felt compelled to build and belong to a tight-knit
community of people, to live healthily, to raise their two
kids in a place where other caring adults and Christian
families could be nearby and part of their lives. Kay and
Matthew were wanting to use their country home and
resources in a way that was perhaps more meaningful,
to take risks and trust God in taking them, and to invite
others into their lives more closely. That was the background, Kay tells us, that led to what the two couples are
planning and doing now.

She tells us there's going to be another home and there's
going to be a farm. Here are the details they know at the
moment: she and Matthew are going to build a second
house on their land, and they're going to start putting the
land to use through agriculture and farming. Along with
that, Kyle and Marie are, in the middle of the worst local
housing market in decades, going to put their home on
the market so their family can move into house number
two. The two families plan to build a barn and get animals;
they also want to learn ways to survive off the local land.
And they're going to care about each other's families with
intent: spending time together, concerning themselves with
each other's kids, sharing resources when needed, having
some sort of accountability in how they're spending money,

and together building and tending one massive plot of vegetables.

On paper it is maybe foolish and a little crazy. Still, to watch the light in their eyes during the talk of these plans—plans of committing to one another for decades, of working to know one another deeply, of learning to depend on each other when cars break down or tragedy hits or just when the flour runs out and another half cup is needed for the recipe; plans of encouraging each other's marriages and investing in each other's kids, of blurring the lines between "my" and "your" material stuff, of digging hands and trowels into the dirt together and tending a garden—it's enough to make any sane person at least a little tipsy on the vision. This is relevant because of the story's final particular as it stands. Which is, Kay tells us: the four of them want to know if the rest of us want in.

There are lots of details yet to be figured out, Kay says, and the K&Ms would like all those who continue in this group to figure out those details together. She says there will be a meeting next Sunday for anybody who's interested. And "interested," she says, means being willing to potentially move out to the country, hopefully within a half mile of where we're all sitting, and agreeing to live in community—that's how she says it, "living in community"—with the others who will be here. There is one couple who seems immediately on board, despite the potential obstacles that exist for their family. The couple is none other than Jenny and Joe.

My first thought is, *But I'm not a hippie.*

Followed by: *Good grief, are my friends hippies?*

Thirdly: *Obviously, I don't know these people well enough.*

It's true, I don't. It is still unclear to me, for instance, whether Kay and Matthew have five kids or four.

The next thing I think about is work, which seems like the hugest, most obvious reason of all for saying no to this. Moving out to the country, even out to the closest edge of a half-mile radius, would extend my workday commute by forty minutes. I can't see how I can afford an extra three hours of driving each week while also staying committed to my job and my manuscript, both of which I feel called and compelled to do. On top of that, if a book deal comes through, I'll need to write even more than I'm writing already. I will need to be hermit-like and in front of my laptop as much as I can. Should a publishing opportunity arise, how excited about community and extra commuting would I be?

But. Farm animals, finances, healthy food, and keeping my six friends—that's a lot of singular Things happening together. The magnitude, combined with the unlikely probability of their convergence, is leading me to believe that either (1) it is supremely, divinely orchestrated or (2) I'm about to make my decision like a total raving lunatic.

By the next Sunday evening, I have begun to suspect that this community invitation could have something to do with the love of God that surpasses all knowledge. I have begun to be convinced that a pair of sturdy rubber boots will be justifiable, as footwear purchases go.

Take Me or Leave Me

THE CURRENT WINTER

BEFORE I CAN officially commit to the farm and such, there are two internal turmoils that must be discussed with the others. While it's great thinking about life's poetry and dreaming about what a community could be, there are still obstacles. Namely, work and money. There is too much of the first, and of the second there might not be enough.

I feel compelled to tell the others about the turmoils. When news like this is left for a late-in-the-game disclosure, it's likely to result in strife or burned bridges, even among cool and forgiving folks like the Ks, the Ms, and the Js. And though I don't have the first practical clue about "living in community," I have an idea that hostility among members isn't a major ingredient they're looking to include in the recipe. Plus, if I were them, I would want the opportunity to rescind my invitation.

From my perspective, everything hinges on initiating a Serious Conversation with the K&Ms and the Js about renting, farm responsibilities, and my overworked, nonprofit-salary reality. I fret about this. I number crunch. I fret and number crunch and pray and fret some more. Finally, at one of our Sunday night meetings at Kay and Matthew's house, I anxiously bring up the issues and also painstakingly lay out the details as I see them.

I lead with the reality that moving out to the farm will add an extra thousand miles in fuel expenses to my monthly budget, which is regularly strained already. I tell my friends I don't know what to think about that, since I don't want to get a different day job and since I'm already moonlighting a manuscript. . . .

I add that if my book proposal eventually gets an editorial bite and a publishing contract, then for at least several months I'll essentially be working two full-time jobs: church by day, book by night. Which for at least several months would render me a worthless community member and a useless farmhand, even in the area of my supposed specialty, the chicken coop. . . .

I offer some of the figures I've come up with, which are: if I eliminate almost all restaurant meals from my budget and plan to not buy any new clothes ever, and if no emergency expenses come up, and if I could find a place near the farm where rent is similar to my current payment (read: nonprofit-appropriate), maybe I could swing the move without going into the red. Barely . . .

I tell them I want to be part of the farm. I tell them how

much they mean to me already and that I want to have the chance to mean something along with them. . . .

I reiterate and reiterate how much I don't want to inconvenience anybody. I make sure I've painted an adequate picture of what in-the-office writing and book writing would mean for me; in particular, I emphasize the moodiness and antisocial-ness that together they might bring.

Then, the confessions made and the frets brought out into the open, I wait to find out whether my friends will take me or leave me. I figure it would only be fair—it would make sense—if here and now they benevolently and benignly left me.

But they are on board, all three couples. They are so on board it almost makes me wonder whether they listened at all to the points of my mini-speech. After what I just said, how could they legitimately come up with enthusiasm like this?

Jenny and Joe tell me they love that the farm could be the place where I finish the book. Marie is excited and suggests that in heavy writing times the others could take on more crop and animal responsibilities. Matthew says they wouldn't expect help from me if a book contract happened; in that case, my most valuable contribution to the farm would be me. "If this is what God has for you to do," Kyle tells me, "then we all want to help you do it." "The farm could be your soft place to fall," Kay says. Everybody else nods and smiles, eyebrows raised hopefully. I sit there wordless and blinking.

But there is still more. Kay and Matthew have been talking about some extra space in their basement, they say;

they'd like to drywall and carpet it so it can be a bedroom
for me to stay in. As for rent, they're not looking for an
extra monthly check to cash. It will help put this home to
good use, they tell me, if I would agree to live here at no
charge. And they see no need for me to pay utilities, since
one more person in the house doesn't make that much difference on the water and electricity bills anyway. And they'd
love to have me join their family around the dinner table
every night. "I'm cooking anyway," Kay says, laughing. If
I wanted to, I could buy and prepare a few meals a month
to share, but there would be no expectation. It would
be great if I could use my leftover would-have-been rent
money to pay off my remaining college loans, or if I could
give it to somebody in need, they say.

I blink again, stunned.

There's a certain wooziness that accompanies grace.
That much I know. It's the feeling of being bowled over by
generosity and simultaneously being gut-certain you don't
come close to deserving it. It's the kind of feeling that can
leave one awed and overjoyed in an instant, that can throw
legitimate doubts and fears out the window.

So I turn ecstatic. I let myself get lost in thoughts of
winter on the farm, with drifting snow and crisp, open air.
I think with no small level of romance about its long driveway lined by old-fashioned lanterns on each side and about
how the place sits on a rectangle of land formed by four
country roads, three paved and one gravel. I look around
and breathe in—there's a fire going in the fireplace, and
the whole house smells like cherry wood and baking. It is
unadorned and lively. There is simplicity and hard work
and restfulness in every direction. I've been told that in the

summer I'll see wildflowers everywhere, in dense clumps that in places are taller than me. I've been told we'll have fireflies all over.

Giddy and smitten, I think that this farm and these people might be the perfect fit: the fullness I didn't know I was asking God for. I remember all the wonderful things that accompany an experience of grace, and I am transfixed because here it is happening again.

As I drive away from the farm that evening, I am thinking about how this farm country is even less populated than Smallertown, that the place probably has a ridiculous festival or two of its own, that surely the fertilizer stench is worse around here. I am proud of myself for being willing to accept these things, for being willing to leave my sleek, twentysomething apartment and start living an unglamorous life here on this plot of farmland with families and animals and dirt. All of this, I am thinking, might be evidence that suggests I'm wiser and more mature than I used to be. I find myself reassured by this thought. It seems to me there's nothing left to do but finalize my plans to move in.

What I don't think about until much later are some of the finer points. Like the wrenching difficulty that tends to accompany grace. Like the many pesky and terrible changes one single grace experience might demand of me. Like how for all its poetic fittedness, grace can also feel far too snug for comfort. Like how there's already an example of extrasnugness here: the KMJs and I have decided that after the necessary barn cats, the first animals to be installed on the farm should be sheep.

Part Two

WITHOUTING

Waiting on Change

PROJECTS RELATED TO the community and the farm start coming together almost immediately. What I find is that while Kyle and Marie, Jenny and Joe, and Kay and Matthew are methodical, practical, think-it-through people, they move at the daring speed of dreamers. In a matter of weeks, they have all begun taking complicated, potentially costly, long-term risks. Their quickness in all of it almost seems rash at times, but apparently they were serious about the whole community and farming thing.

Kay and Matthew have completed a process of surveying and mapping their property's soil and drainage patterns. They've secured building permits and broken ground for farmhouse number two, and they've drywalled and carpeted that brand-new basement bedroom. Marie and Kyle have put their home in town—the home that just months ago they were planning to live in for decades—on the market. Jenny and Joe, after having their house snatched up almost the moment a For Sale sign went up out front, have moved their family of six into a short-term rental, are making an offer on a house next door to the farm, and are considering switching their kids to a different school system midyear.

Joe is in the process of switching his schedule toward less overtime so he can help work the farm. Marie has built a timeline for resigning from her corporate position so she can manage the garden project and canning. Matthew is cutting back his hours at the office so he can have more to give on the property too. All three families are expecting major income and lifestyle changes, and they are planning to live far more simply, all in order to work the farm and to make the place a joint effort.

As for me, I have given my roommate notice that I'll be moving out, I have thought about packing up some of my stuff at the condo, and I have picked a paint color for the farmhouse basement bedroom. Compared to sacrifices and contributions being made by the others, these seem watered down and wimpy. I feel guilty about that, so I throw myself into doing the one useful thing I can do: I write. I write as much and as quickly as I can, with hopes that someday when I get to the farm, there will be little writing left to do and I'll be able to pull my own weight in the community.

I write and write, so much that I manage to complete the outline and sample chapters I've been working toward. Next I send what I have to a literary agent, who responds positively. A couple of days later we have a phone conversation, and I can tell that not only does he know the world of publishing like a pro, he's also not the sort to put up with bellyaching or nonsense. I like him immediately. The agent agrees to represent me, and after some tweaks to the manuscript, he sends it to several of his contacts. Thus begins a period of time with some extra breathing room.

For a while there is no work that can or should be done on the book. I fill hours by catching up with friends, cooking, watching movies, and reading. Then I add packing up and purging my stuff, taking walks to the library, and working extra hours at the office. I buy a throw pillow to match the color of the farmhouse basement bedroom. I take some naps. After a bit of this, I begin to have bouts of boredom and restlessness.

In the middle of this—also, notably, in the middle of a novel about a couple named Marshall and Leigh—I am matched up, I admit, by an online dating service. The person I am matched with is a man named Marshall, and he is not only good looking and over six feet tall but also bookish, funny, insightful, and seemingly interested in me. Yes, I am slightly embarrassed about the online dating service part, but the point is, it was a free ten-day trial offer that arrived in my in-box on an especially lackluster day. The point is, what did I have to lose? The point is, my best friends from college still call me Leigh, and *What are the chances,* I keep telling myself, *of a name coincidence like that?*

Within the confines of the online dating portal, e-Marshall and I exchange exactly a dozen messages before I start developing a crush on his bio. He's three years older than me, a runner, and a reader, and he's working on his master's degree. I choose to overlook that he's somewhat grandiose in his adoration of coffee; this, because he also has good taste in novelists, loves the city of Boston, and tutors kids for a living (his grammar is impeccable). From the photos I've seen, e-Marshall looks like the kind of guy you'd expect to become a professor, a well liked one. Also I know that he grew up in the Midwest, in farm country, and that he has a brother whose family lives just thirty minutes away from my apartment.

(Interruptive note: My first thought on learning about the Michigan relatives is that they could be a standing and automatic excuse for e-Marshall to visit town, which could be a convenient and nonchalant way for him to suggest we should meet. A relationship, finally. *Charmed, I'm sure.*)

Saying that I want him to be interested in me doesn't express it fully. I want him to be more than interested. I want, a couple months from now, to be able to tell him and everybody about the intersection of fiction Marshall and Leigh and real-life Marshall and Leigh, and I want to be able to smile with him and tell him that at the start of it all I wondered if this was Providence. Because there's a chance I could actually be compatible with an academic guy like this. Certainly the odds here and now are better than they would be with one of the—*ahem*—less intellectual types who tend to pose oiled and shirtless for their profile pictures. And e-Marshall contacted me, so the hopes I have are not entirely fabricated this time. He made the first move, which gives this some actual substance. It's no small deal, I tell myself, that here we are several weeks later, going e-strong.

As if the online flirtation isn't enough—and I'm thinking it *is* enough—there's fantastic news in the publishing world too. My agent checks in to say that he's hearing good feedback. He thinks we can be confident something will happen.

So I wait on two counts, and I float on two counts too. Changes feel so close on the horizon and so sure to me that I can practically touch them. A real love interest, a contracted book project. I have been working toward the latter for two years, and I have been hoping for the former since well before puberty. Which is why, in the midst of my exuberance and girly besottedness, the thought that comes to me most frequently is *Somehow, some way, do not screw this up*. Which is, I should know by now, a sign that I've already screwed it up in the biggest way possible.

God as a Vegetable

IN THE FIRST week of the Honey Project, the way I tried to explain the fast to my friend Cora was in the language of hardy greens. "If it were up to me to cram God into a flavor," I told her, "I would've picked something like asparagus." God is sturdy and good for a person—that's how this metaphor worked itself out. God should be a regular part of somebody's intake. God should be the source of energy and strength. It would make sense that parents would feed God to their kids, that people would tell their friends about him. Asparagus, I told Cora. The obvious problem being, earlier that day I had been pining for saltwater taffy and peanut M&M'S, not vegetable stalks.

It was a Tuesday evening. I was on a several-day streak

of being sweets obsessed, with no signs of fading. Cora and I were talking on the phone, which by then was something we had been doing weekly for a couple of years. In fact, had it not been for our scheduled phone call that evening and the questions I knew Cora would pose, I probably would've caved to my cravings a few potential snack breaks earlier.

Her main question that night was the same one we had been asking each other every Tuesday evening: "How's your relationship with God?" Our pattern in answering that question was (and still is) to talk about the week just passed. That night, however, when Cora asked me about my relationship with God, the only response I could think of was about fasting. Really, it was a response about everything. A tall green plant, I told her, one with semi-prickly shoots.

Cora and I met while I was in college. She was in her midforties, married to Jack, a religion prof at the university I attended. She had no kids but two teenage nieces to dote on. Cora wore no makeup and pulled her hair into a bun every day of the week. At the time I was trying very hard to be a laid-back, fashionable college student who always remembered perfume and lip gloss and eyeliner too. But one Sunday afternoon, at a church potluck lunch that I hadn't really wanted to go to in the first place, Cora and I ended up sitting beside each other, talking about teenagers and about Hebrew 200.

She liked that I had done some speaking at seminars for teens; she thought maybe I could mentor her nieces. I liked that she had eagerly audited the Hebrew class on campus; I thought maybe here was someone who would be excited about biblical words and languages with me. It was one of those rare occasions when two people understand and care about each other almost immediately.

When I wasn't able to squeeze any Hebrew into my upcoming spring term, Cora offered to teach me the basics. She said it would give her an incentive to stay brushed up on vocab. I think she was mostly being nice. But either way, a few weeks later the two of us started meeting in my dorm lobby on Sunday afternoons to sound out Old Testament verb forms. From the beginning, the study was about more than language for both of us; we wanted ways to know God and learn the Bible deeply, to discover prayer and uncover faith within ourselves. It was one of the most plainly spiritual things I did all year.

For the remaining semesters until I graduated, Cora and I kept meeting, and later when I moved back north to Michigan, we stayed in touch. Then a point came when we decided to talk with each other every week, so I started calling her every Tuesday at 7 p.m. on my cell plan's free minutes. We began our pattern of talking about what God had been teaching us, about where we were falling short, and about what decisions and struggles we were facing. Then we'd pray for each other and hang up.

It was then, and it is now, just one hour—one phone call a week. In times when we've been busy, sometimes it hasn't even been that. Our friendship was four years old when I realized the oddity of it: I had stepped inside her house only once, and she had never glimpsed my apartment. Still, of all the people whose days intersect mine, Cora is one who knows me better than most anybody else. Many times over the years she has helped spur me on and revive my reasons for believing in belief.

On the night of the asparagus discussion, however, I didn't feel spurred or revived. This had nothing to do with Cora; rather, I was sugar starved and love jealous, dissatisfied with my career, loaded with debt (three grand to Visa), and freshly rejected by UC. Everything felt dark and cavernous and hungry; it was a physical, emotional, spiritual appetite all in one. I was sulky and sad. I was on the brink, too, of feeling sorrier for myself than I had ever felt. I know this because while reading my Bible in the evenings, I had begun to read from the book of Job. No other part of Scripture seemed to have the potential to connect. In Job, I paged through chapter after chapter and verse after verse of disasters and boils and smiting, and I felt strangely comforted. My own difficulties weren't nearly as intense as the ones I was reading about; still, *Job*, I had been telling myself, *now* there's *some misery I can relate to.*

So that night when Cora asked, like always, about my relationship with God, what I said was, "I don't know. . . ." I let the response trail off. Then I sighed. For a long time there was silence on the line as I thought about the question.

This is what I thought about: Since as far back as I could remember, a spiritual life had been central and meaningful to me. My entire history—friends, education, choices, behaviors, goals—had been an attempt to bring my life in line with what God had asked of me. The things I did were the things a Christian girl was supposed to do; the things I avoided were things all the staunchest church ladies said you were wise to avoid. A careful life like that was the kind of life I had come to prefer, so it didn't bother me when my peers didn't entirely understand me. Everything within me said I was following the right beat: God seemed close and my youth pastors told me I was amazing. Later in life, consistently doing the right thing had become a calling card of sorts for me and even a residual writing income. The religious subculture perks continued.

But as I sat there that night with the phone at my ear, I was also thinking about a different reality: namely, that for a while now my familiar, youth-group-approved kind of living hadn't been enough. A dozen or so Saturdays a year, moms who didn't know me were lining up with their daughters at afternoon seminars, asking me to sign copies of my book and telling me I was a role model. Yet in the midst of it, God seemed far off—miles away—and unfeeling. The heat that had once filled my relationship with him was escaping, like somebody had left a door open somewhere and it was getting drafty in here.

"How do you think your life would change if God became the sweetness in it?" Cora asked me then.

I thought about this. I thought about Ray's story of the rabbi dripping honey on squares of waxed paper, about the kids leaning forward in their seats, about how honey used to be decadence, the sweetest taste people knew. Then I told her I didn't have a clue. She has been asking incredible questions like that nearly every week since the first letter of the Hebrew alphabet.

Sam James, the Wrong Guy

THREE WINTERS AGO

THERE ARE RELIGIOUS PEOPLE, married ones, who make a habit of telling their single friends that romance comes around "when you become totally content with Jesus" or "when you stop thinking about a relationship and commit yourself fully to God" or "when you give up trying and instead trust the Lord to find your man for you." This is slot-machine theology: drop in your coin, pull the crank, and expect that in no time God will send clinking down into that little tray exactly the kind of jackpot life you've ordered. It is biblically unfounded, pompous fiction. Still, by the third week of the Honey Project, I was almost willing to consider it.

Not that I thought I had become totally content or

that I was suddenly 100 percent committed to God, and not that I had thrown in the towel on trying for a relationship. But for twenty-some days, I *had* successfully given up chocolate, desserts, and every other kind of sweet. As far as spiritual commitment goes, I figured that wasn't too shabby. And for the first time in my life, wonder of wonders, it actually seemed feasible that I might have a real, non-blind date. And this wasn't just some mirage I had cooked up in my head; the guy seemed like he might be genuinely interested. It was unprecedented.

The man's name was Sam James. He was a graphic designer and an excellent dresser whom I had met a few weeks earlier. He had picked up his little sister at a youth retreat where I was the speaker, and after introducing himself to me, he didn't run away like the wind, even though I was standing next to a few stacks of *Saving My First Kiss*. This practically knocked all the air out of my respiratory system. Then I was pulled away and he walked to another corner of the room to talk with a few more people, but out of the corner of my eye I noticed he was keeping his shoulders slightly open toward me, even in the midst of those other conversations. I had seen guys take that stance plenty of times before, only I had always been the one they were turned slightly away from while they focused their real attention on someone else. But Sam James was looking at me.

He hung around for a while, apparently waiting for another chance for us to talk, and then sauntered over with a smile and a business proposition. He needed some writing updated on his website, he said. Would I consider meeting him for coffee and suggesting a new approach?

I stunned myself by being able to say, "Sure, that would be great," with a semblance of composure. I gave him my email address without giggling like a schoolgirl.

A week later we met for coffee and laughed a lot and talked about business only a little. Two weeks after that, we were sending each other multiple emails per hour, enough for me to have amassed a fairly extensive bio for Sam James. I knew his basic family info, schooling, church history, preferred clichés, clothing style, and vehicle make and model. I knew he frequently used frown-face emoticons in his emails. He liked to host friends at his house. He was organizationally scattered and had fascinating stories from a variety of unique experiences. He was atrocious with spelling. He had the curious habit of signing his initials at the end of every email message, even at the end of one- or two-word instant replies. Sometimes he double-initialed: once before the PS and again after it. Sometimes he seemed too interested in talking about himself, but then again, he was interesting, so maybe it was okay. He was thinking of moving to Seattle, for instance.

I decided I was willing to consider becoming Northwestern.

Then one day Sam James called to say he was having a meeting with clients in my neighborhood on Friday evening, and how about if he stopped over at my place afterward with a bottle of wine? I said, "Sure, I'd love to," and when we hung up I had to peel myself off the ceiling. All I could think was, *Date, date, date, date, date.* This would be a date! Wine equaled a date. Friday night equaled a date. Just the two of us, prearranged by him, equaled a date. Definitely. Finally!

In the days leading up to Friday, even a dead-end outcome seemed promising. If Sam James didn't turn out to be lasting romance, at a minimum I'd get to stop being the dateless wonder I had always been. I would be Somebody Who Dates. I could expect at least that, I had thought.

Hey Lisa,

So . . . just realised my meeting tonigt is at 7. Probably wont be done til 830. ☹ OK with you if I come over at 9 instead? Sorry . . .

SJ

It was Friday afternoon, and Sam James was changing plans just hours in advance because he had double-booked. He was doing so with three spelling errors, two counts of absent punctuation, and a double showing of ellipses, which in my opinion is a flagrant misuse of periods. Perhaps I should've taken all that as a sign, but I didn't. I focused on the fact that it was about to be Friday night, and I told myself that on a Friday night I should have wine with a man rather than correcting his English in my head. I told myself that Sam James was in need of organization and a little help maintaining his calendar. He was in need of a good woman.

Going home to my apartment after work, I made some brownies and lit a candle in the kitchen. I put some finishing touches on a massive cleaning and tidying project that had commenced the night before, with the aim of domestically impressing Sam James. I had a salad for dinner because it made me feel thin. Then I changed out of my work clothes to put on my favorite jeans, my most casually curve-skimming sweater, and perfume, too. I was ready at 8:30, with a half hour to spare.

9:00, nothing.

9:15, nothing.

9:35, a text message.

hey, two blocks away, going to leaf and be their soon.

9:50, nothing.

10:10, he was seventy minutes late.

10:20, eighty.

10:25, I packaged the brownies and put them away.

I wanted to go to bed or at least stop looking at the clock. I had been up late the night before, after all, scrubbing my bathroom sink and the floor of my shower.

At 10:45, I got a phone call; there was a bass beat drumming in the background. These clients were so great, Sam James told me, I'd love them. The food was great too. People were having a great time, it was great. He said he'd be out the door and on his way over in five minutes, maybe ten. As he told me these things, I had to move the phone away from and then back toward my ear, away from and back toward again, because with each new sentence Sam James's voice was at a different volume than the sentence before. And every sentence was too loud, no matter how close or far away the phone. When the call was over, I stood dazed and stupid in the middle of my living room for several minutes. Had Sam James slurred his words? Surely he hadn't.

The clock in my kitchen read at not quite half an inch away from midnight when he arrived. He had a grin on his face and an unopened bottle of red in hand. He smelled like he had just taken a swim at a brewery.

It was too surprising and too confusing for me to process actual thoughts; reflex and habit took over. I went through the same series of motions I had been practicing with guests for years. Later my brothers and several male friends would lecture me about nearly every part of this: I invited Sam James inside, took his coat, asked if I could get him some water, asked about his day. Then I stood in my kitchen with nothing to say and no ideas about what to do.

The rest of it unfolded like a bad, bad dream sequence, with pieces all mismatched and unsorted. After having been convinced to leave the wine unopened, the corkscrew untouched, Sam James slumped into a seat across from me at the kitchen table. He started talking, and his range of topics (all unmentioned in our relationship until then) included his DUI from the previous month, his poor handling of the legal process that followed, his still-unsettled recent breakup, his frequently unpaid mortgage bills, the senseless purchases he kept making instead, and the expected foreclosure on his house. He talked about the lies he had been telling his parents and friends and how it would be only a matter of time before that work of fiction would cave in too. Then he told me again that the meeting with his clients that night had been great—they really were *so* great. All his talk came at me quickly, end over end, and I didn't have time to concentrate on it until he was done. By that time there was so much to be thought about that zeroing in on any particular land mine was too difficult.

I felt sad for Sam James. I wished I could help him. I wished he would leave. I thought about how handsome he was. I thought, *This man is a terrible speller.* I was mad at him for being late. Glad I hadn't offered him a brownie. Furious I was still fasting from brownies. Irritated he had crafted an image. Angry I had fallen for it. Relieved to know the truth. Mostly, though, I was disappointed that the truth had come out in the way it had. I was disappointed it had come out so quickly.

An innocent glass of wine and some conversation with Sam James would have only delayed and complicated the inevitable; that much was obvious. But a glass of wine and conversation would have been nice for one night. It would have been a date, maybe.

Sam James slumped and talked. I listened and thought. He sobered up. By then it had gotten late and dark. Our eyes were heavy, and when I looked at him it was clear that the magic of What Could Have Been had been spent. I think he knew it too. But politeness and habit kicked in once more: we agreed it was safe for him to drive, I retrieved his coat, he told me I could keep the wine, I said I'd walk him to his car. He held the door open for me as we stepped outside.

There was snow on the ground, a fresh dusting. I knew that in daylight it would be pristine, feathery white. In the darkness, though, it seemed pallid and grayed. Sam James walked beside me, and our footprints made two paths next to each other on the driveway. I glanced down at them and was struck by the thought that they looked like a pair. Side by side and pressed there onto the pavement, they had every appearance of togetherness. Such irony.

When we had parted ways in the past, Sam James had made a point to hug me good-bye. On that night he didn't try. He got into his car and half-waved. I forced a half-smile and stepped away from him, back into the Michigan winter. He turned the key in the ignition, and I wrapped my arms tightly around myself for warmth. As he drove away, it was difficult for me to feel anything but the chill.

The next morning I woke up feeling numb and exhausted. If God had much to do with the escapades of Sam James, I thought, then God was nothing more than an elaborate tease. He had let me get my hopes up that maybe things could be better, then after I fell for the ploy, he jerked me back to status quo. And somehow it was so much worse being back there, having believed in the hope that he might take me somewhere else. I wasn't sure whether God cared how I felt about that—evidence seemed to suggest he might not.

God's silence was confusing and tiring at best. At worst it seemed cruel. It made a not-so-tiny part of me wonder if I had unknowingly gotten off track somewhere. I wondered if maybe this was my deserved punishment, if this was God stepping in and pulverizing things.

Still, for the duration of another day I didn't eat sweets. I walked past a candy dish at the bank. I kept turning down chocolate and declining desserts. I drank water, not soda, not punch. God is not a slot machine, but sometimes it's hard to resist putting in a few extra nickels, just to keep the odds up.

Halfsies

THREE WINTERS AGO

AT THE START of the Honey Project, my overwhelming
response to God was a feeling of betrayal. I felt he had
repeatedly cheated me out of things I deserved—or at the
very least, he had given the things I wanted to pretty much
everybody else but me. I didn't understand why he would
keep doing that. I was one of his children, after all, and I
wasn't a slouch in the role. I obeyed him. I longed to please
and delight him. As a part of his family, I wasn't asking
to be the spoiled favorite, but I felt worthy of something
beyond what felt like scraps. I was sure I had earned more
than just my keep. But as far as I could tell, God wasn't
interested in putting sweetness into my life, at least not the
kind of sweetness I wanted.

Take finances, for instance. Finances had always been difficult. This had little to do with materialism or greed; the problem was that so much of life felt like a constant battle to make ends meet, and it was up to me to manage the meeting. Just me, alone. And, sure, I *could* be materialistic and greedy at times, which only complicated things.

I knew too many people—friends, family members, acquaintances—who not only had more money than I did *and* a spouse to help them earn and handle their finances but also had more than once received large gifts or cash sums to help them get by. I played these peoples' stories over and over in my head, because often the stories included benefactors who had been "told" by God to be so generous. *God told them to give me this car. God told them to give me twelve thousand dollars. God told them to give me an all-expenses-paid month in Bermuda.* As for me, the majority of people seemed to assume I didn't need gifts or assistance of any kind. They seemed to expect that I would be self-sufficient and fine on my own. I had no idea where they were getting this impression, but the fact that they were made me berserk sometimes. Worse than that, though, was the idea that God's arrangement of things had left me as one of the ones who didn't get handouts or freebies. In a frame of awareness that includes human trafficking, world hunger, and cervical cancer, this complaint is obviously ungrateful and petty. But there you have it.

Another thing was my career. I had authored one book and as a ghostwriter was working on a second, which at first glance in the world of writers is something to be jumping-around thrilled about. Most of the time it felt backhanded to me. For instance, whenever people discovered I worked in writing, they would almost 75 percent of the time ask if I'd ever had anything published. Which left me to either lie or go into the whole bit about never been kissed. Which ultimately was a lot of talking with strangers about my not kissing. And the ghostwriting project was a book my two bosses were working on about marriage, which ultimately meant a lot of talking with them about husband-and-wife life and how wonderful it was. As if seven wedding invitations for the upcoming summer weren't already enough.

Which is to say: I was especially indignant that God seemed to be holding out on the category of romance. For over two decades, I had faithfully believed in him and by most standards I had been mostly good—at times I felt I was throwing myself into being good—yet there always seemed to be a shortage of wants granted. It was a simple matter of mismatched proportion. In my eyes, my level of deservingness had always stuck to the high side of the charts, say the ninety-fifth percentile, yet particular asked-for blessings were disproportionately low, say the fifth. It seemed spiteful and unbecoming of him.

My relationship with God, from my perspective, was like this: I put in a hefty effort for him and wanted just some sweet treats every now and then in return. Cash bonuses; admiration from handsome, interested, interesting men; an end to some of the trying. I wasn't asking for all of that at once; God could've started with just one piece, and I would've been elated. But he didn't. I went without.

God withheld, I withouted. That was how things were with us. It seemed it was how it had always been.

The way I saw things, there were only two rational

explanations for all the withholding and the withouting.
Either God wasn't as loving and generous as my Sunday
school lessons claimed he was, or I hadn't yet done enough
to merit his generous gifts. The former would've accounted
for my betrayed feeling, but I knew that believing it
would've amounted to several counts of heresy. Believing
the latter didn't seem quite so likely to end in smiting,
but I couldn't reconcile it with the fact that women who
seemed entirely virtueless were at that very moment married, copulating, professionally successful, jeweled, fashionable, rich. All this confused me tremendously.

Of the scenarios to choose from, I couldn't let myself
believe either one—they were both so perturbing—but
I couldn't think of any other possibilities. In the end,
I believed neither, and I half-believed both.

I half-believed that God was unfeeling about me or on
some kind of power trip. Because of this, I stopped asking
him for the things I wanted most. I figured he was God; he
knew already. It felt safer to close off that portion of myself.
To make the request, to extend it in my hands and ask that
God notice, would stir it to life. It meant risking that he
would ignore the request entirely. If a prayer is sent out and
repeatedly left unanswered, it can begin to seem that God
is silent, absent, even cruel. And then what do you do?

I half-believed that I simply hadn't done enough yet,
hadn't earned enough points to make it to the prize round.
Because of this, I worked even harder at things that seemed
spiritually pleasing and impressive. When the Honey
Project began, I half-gladly said no to most of my favorite
foods. I thought of God whenever I thought of sweets,
which was often. On good days I woke up early to read my

Bible and pray. I half-had nice and fluffy thoughts about God. I held out half-hope that someday it would all be enough. God would notice my effort and devotion, and he would see that it was true; he would be satisfied and start making changes in my life that were to my liking.

The half-beliefs were my foundation. I built faith upon them like a house, and I lived there for a long time. Then came a realization of God's grace. It was the best of good news, and at the same time it was as if a quake had cracked the walls and blasted canyons in the cement of everything. All I had and all I was, was rubble.

I know now that to put faith on anything but the gospel of grace is to live on a fault line. The bedrock anywhere else is shifty underneath, and the structure above can't hold. Grace is the one foundation that's solid all the way to the bottom, immovable. It's the only safe and forever trustworthy place on which to build.

That being said, the fault line was home to me once. Even after everything, I find it's an easy comfort to want to go back to.

E-Flirting

THE CURRENT WINTER

I HAVE BECOME agitated and impatient about Marshall. The details he has chosen to share about himself and his life, though a fine collection, have after several weeks started to seem not only scant and somewhat shallow but also costly, considering that he and I are both paying a fee in monthly installments to write each other like this. He hasn't yet told me his last name or which school he's attending for his master's, he hasn't divulged any real specifics about his work or family or beliefs, and the closest he's come to sharing an opinion has been recommending a musician by way of YouTube video links. I watch one song from a live concert, and I can't imagine enjoying it under any circumstance.

Still, I have been holding back from asking for details

and getting personal. I have been reminding myself that a connection might not happen right away, and I have been telling myself I can be satisfied with chitchat for a while. All this requires repeated valiant efforts, not to mention extensive deleting in my messages; still, it works long enough in each instance for me to click Send without making a fool of myself. The catch, however, is that this self-control in writing has been offset by boy-crazed sense-lessness elsewhere. Particularly: I have been overtalking the Marshall situation with my roommate, overanalyzing him on the phone with my sister, checking obsessively for messages on the online dating site, crying in unreasonable amounts when nothing from him is there, and brainstorm-ing passive-aggressive ways I might manipulate this almost-stranger into a relationship.

Beyond his taste in music, what confuses me about Marshall is that he keeps writing me while also seeming perfectly content with our being mostly uninformed about each other. I want to know: Is he interested, or is he just filling empty time? (If he's not interested, wouldn't he sim-ply stop writing? And if he is interested, wouldn't he write more often?) Before his most recent message to me, he allowed a weeklong gap in communication; this was *after* I had apologized for taking two days to respond to him. The apology was part sincere, part test.

So eight emails in, I am ignoring that the pattern of e-Marshall's correspondence with me has slowed: on each of the first few days he sent multiple messages, but soon after that he began taking a full day or even two or three to write again. I am ignoring the apparent disinterest, rude-ness, and/or absentmindedness this pattern might suggest.

I am also ignoring that the fictitious Marshall and Leigh broke up in chapter 11. I refrain from asking myself which is more pathetic: that I'm willing to be strung along by a guy who may or may not be vaguely interested in me, or that I know it.

At the five-week point in our correspondence, while driving home from work after another day without a message from e-Marshall, I imagine myself not as myself but as his trusted and strictly platonic female confidant. In this scenario, he meekly comes to me for advice about interacting with a certain redheaded writer whom he met online and finds fascinating and ravishingly beautiful. He admits he hasn't taken the next step toward making it a relationship, and he asks the imagined-adviser me how long he should wait before doing so. In my imagined role what I suggest he should do is "Pee or get off the pot."

In actual, non-imagined life, I am far less definitive and eloquent. What I do is walk through the front door and ask my roommate, Courtney, if I should email him again or if I should wait some more.

"When was the last time he wrote you?" she asks.

"Last Monday." It is currently day nine of Hearing Nothing from Marshall Again.

"And you responded on Wednesday?"

Yes, two days later I tried to be alluring and apologized for taking so long.

"And there wasn't anything weird about his message?"

I tell her that it was long and funny and interesting.

I tell her he seemed the same and that he had asked questions.

I ask her if I'm crazy.

She pauses, and in that moment of quiet I begin fearing she's the friend who lost the straw poll and now has to be the one to break the harsh and embarrassing truth to me—something like: *Lisa, you long ago hiked to the peak of the Marshall molehill.* But Courtney doesn't make any such implication; rather, she is gracious. She is practical and realistic, even hopeful. She says no; she can't make any sense of the guy either.

For a while we sit in the living room of our apartment, trying to figure out both men in general and this one specifically. We don't make progress. We decide that if love were a sports team and men had to try out for a chance to play, then Marshall has just been demoted to second-string JV. We decide that I should wait five more days, until the waiting amounts to an inexcusable total of two weeks. We decide that after that point I will not contact him again; I will cut him from the team. I tell myself I can be determined enough to manage that. I *can.*

Later that same evening, I spend at least an hour crafting in my head an elaborate and brilliant message to Marshall. The strategy behind it is to (1) playfully inform him that I'd like to hear from him more often, while also (2) successfully not sounding pitiful.

After an hour of mental wording and paragraphing, I admit to myself that the content is built on nothing but cheap compliments and veiled requests. It is, even in theory, obvious desperation and impending disaster.

I try praying about the Marshall situation and about what I should do. I want the prayer to be contrite and genuine, but instead it starts out petty and turns into a gripe. I tell God I'm annoyed with myself for not knowing whether this guy is someone I should give a second thought to, and I tell him I'm sick of feeling lost and juvenile about every man who becomes something of a presence in my life. I speculate to God that this is quickly shaping up to be no different from most every other time before, when I've fallen for somebody only to find that the interest isn't reciprocated and the joke is on me. I point out that the fact that I still haven't had a boyfriend at twenty-seven years old is getting ridiculous. I remind God that he's God and that he could've easily changed things a long time ago if he'd wanted to.

I end the prayer. I don't type my brilliant, whiny message to e-Marshall, and I don't send it either. I go to bed full of sighs.

For a few nights in a row, I get out of bed at least once before falling asleep to check my Marshall-free in-box, and in the middle of the night I wake up once more to fitfully check it again. After a while I start wondering whether there will come a day when the guy simply forgets to respond to me. Which after several weeks and a couple more messages, he does.

Prayer by Typo

THE CURRENT WINTER

LATE ONE AFTERNOON I get a call from a big-time editor who has been reviewing my manuscript submission for a while. My pulse quickens as I pick up the phone.

The first time this particular editor called and dropped the name of her publishing house, I reached a point that was very close to salivating. Some of the authors associated with the place are my writing heroes, so when it seemed possible I might join their ranks, I became inordinately preoccupied with the idea of being that cool. The next-best thought on my mind was that of one day leading with a title other than *Saving My First Kiss* when people asked me if I'd been published. And maybe, I thought, this could be a step toward becoming a full-time book writer instead

of needing an office job too. Because while writing manu-
scripts is a lovely, dreamy way to spend one's days, a girl
needs to buy insurance and pay rent. For that, publishing
contracts are required. Hence my raised heart rate the next
time the editor's number appears on caller ID.

Up till now, all signs have been pointing to good news:
Ms. Editing claimed to like the submission a lot, she said
her whole reviewing team likes it too, and she has even
invested time in talking through my outline with me as if
it were her project already. She made a point to meet me
and buy me breakfast, she discussed necessary business, she
emailed to say, "Finally I have news! Let's talk!" and, yes, in
her email she used exclamation points.

My agent expects we'll get an offer. My writer friends are
thinking it's a done deal. I am already picturing this publisher's logo on my book's back cover: instant credibility. I
am thinking of all the authors with whom I'll have that logo
in common, and I am hoping we'll all be instant chums.

I answer the editor's phone call. It is a brief conversation, a flat no with little explanation. I am so stunned
afterward that it takes ten minutes before I start falling
apart. Then I cry and feel exhausted, and I get slightly furious at God for being so elusive with his plan for this supposed calling. Here I have been obedient and committed
to a project for years, literally years. I have sacrificed my
friendships and my free time and my rest, all to do what he
seemed to ask. Isn't there something to be said for that? Yet
my best efforts aren't measuring up, and who knows how
many untold months and tedious drafts it'll take before
there's a chance like this again.

A week after the rejection, I'm in charge of leading

our Wednesday morning prayer session at the office. The church staff gathers in a room, and I'm to guide us all through some Scripture verses, prayers, and meditation for a half hour. We'll close by saying the Lord's Prayer together, then we'll get back to work. It's nothing complicated, and to help keep it simple for people, I've prepped a nifty half-page handout of the readings and prayers we'll be using. I am somewhat proud of those little sheets, I admit. The margins and fonts are especially well formatted.

We meet. We pray and read. At the end of the half hour, as people are filing out of the room, I start gathering up the leftover printouts. In doing this, I glance down at one of the copies, and my eyes immediately zero in on a mistake. It's in the first two lines of the Lord's Prayer. The way I typed the lines, they read:

Our Father, who art in Heaven,

Hollowed be your name.

Hollowed. I feel my cheeks flush, and I lament once again that word processing programs can't yet spell-check based on context. Hollowed. As in hollowing out a canoe. As in yelling across the hollows. As in promises that are hollow. Not sacred, divine, and *hallowed.* No, *hollowed*: made empty and dull.

It isn't often that a misspelling causes a spiritual break-through in my life, but on this day it does. It stops me. Reading *hollowed* on the page—hollowed be our Father's name—I realize that there's far more to it than just a letter *o* where the *a* should be.

I don't have a book deal. I'm twenty-seven years old, and I don't have a boyfriend, never have. I don't even have somebody stringing me along. All that is part of it, but there is so much more.

My baby brother, David, now a full-fledged Marine, is training to deploy to a combat zone affectionately known as IED Alley. That would be Improvised Explosive Devices, roadside bombs. My baby brother. My grandma is old and sick and dying. And for months I've been pulling myself away from friends and family in order to write—I haven't been shy about announcing this; I've never been able to keep my mouth shut when I'm hopeful—and now the submission has been rejected and everybody will know. And I still can't be social because there's still no book contract, and without a contract for this blasted calling, I still won't feel free to see people. And I'm tired and worn because every day all the time I am working. And lately how I feel about God is wasteland-hollow.

Compared to three years ago, much is different. I'm not forgetting that. But much is the same, and I've started to wonder again whether God is the withholding type. I've started to feel again like I'm withouting. There are still so many corners of my life where I'm not happy, where I'm disappointed, where I'm afraid. I have the familiar old questions: How can he be trustworthy? How can he possibly care? If he were and if he did, wouldn't he want to make it better? And how, with so much substance gone out of one's faith, can she find a way to get some back?

Faith Playing Fair

THREE WINTERS AGO

IT IS TELLING, I think, that my plan at the beginning of the Honey Project went far beyond fasting. My plan was to fast and then some. I intended to spend six months pulling out all the spiritual stops and making myself incredibly deserving. I wanted the fast to be as striking as possible, not to mention brilliantly executed. To that end, the agenda included:

- Read the Bible daily, several chapters.
- Bible reading doesn't count if it takes place only in bed during the last five minutes before/while falling asleep.
- Tithing is a necessity.

- Pray daily, preferably more than once.
- Prayers should be more than just selfishly asking for things—try listening, too, for a change.
- Prayers should also include thankfulness and praise—more of that than the selfishly asking for things.
- As with Bible reading, prayers don't count if at any point there is dozing off, and especially not if there is dozing off while selfishly asking for things.
- It's okay to ask for things that aren't selfish.
- Memorize Scripture, multiple chapters.
- Do not eat sweets.
- Do *not* eat *any* sweets.

The making of the list was far easier than the keeping of it. Although I repeatedly insisted to myself that certainly I should be able to follow each and every stipulated item, by the time the third month rolled around, I had begun thinking success wasn't likely. I had failed, either partially or totally, on every bullet point except the last two. Which is to say that the only fasting goal I was managing to meet was fasting itself. The others I did occasionally if I was lucky. I memorized some Bible verses, for instance.

Leaving such an important list so largely undone had me feeling guilt ridden and foolish much of the time. I kept feeling that way, even long after giving up on most of the list. The remorse was probably justified, I figured. It was like some form of penance for my lack of discipline, for my overall laziness. *Here I am,* I thought, *claiming I want God to show me he's honey, yet I'm not even willing to do the exemplary things that might attract his extra attention.* How

could I expect him to be especially moved? How could
I ask him to respond sweetly?

It was sometime around nine or ten weeks into fasting
when my questions and theories fell apart. At that point
I was still reading from the book of Job—Job, because all
the wretched miserableness of it still seemed appropriate,
and also because I hadn't been keeping bullet one: Read the
Bible daily, several chapters.

My skimpy Scripture-reading schedule had brought me
only about three-quarters of the way through the book. I
had read the brief introduction of the character Job, which
says he is "blameless—a man of complete integrity,"[1] that
he fears God and stays away from evil. Immediately after
that I read about the start of the misery, which begins
right away, still in chapter 1. Job is made to endure the
loss of his livestock and most of his servants (by theft and
by firestorm), then the loss of all his children (a house col-
lapses on them). In chapter 2, things don't get better. Job
is inflicted with painful sores, head to toe. The Bible says
these things happen—blight after havoc after disaster after
catastrophe, all in one sole life—because God allows them.

In the chapters that immediately follow, a few of Job's
friends (who at first were speechless and cried at the sight
of him) give off-kilter spiritual commentaries about his
string of tragic happenings. One friend says that Job is
being punished for sin and that if he wants stuff to stop
disappearing and people to stop dying, he should confess.
Another friend advises Job to listen to people who are older
and wiser than he is, insinuating the problem is that Job is
some kind of young punk. A third implies there's no way
Job is blameless, no way his heart is committed to God. If

those things were true, the friend says, then circumstances wouldn't be awful anymore.

Job responds by anguishing about his life and lamenting his friends' so-called devotion, but mostly he responds with prayer. He responds with confidence, both in God and in himself. "I know that my Redeemer lives," Job says, "and that in the end he will stand on the earth."[2] He says, "Let God weigh me in honest scales and he will know that I am blameless."[3] After this, Job gets hit with another pile of slams and criticisms. Eventually his patience seems to crack a little, and he becomes more insistent that he hasn't done anything to deserve what's happening to him.

In reading all this, I was sympathetic to Job. I didn't see any reason to hold it against him when he started strongly asking God to explain things; as far as I could tell, that part seemed perfectly logical and justified. To my thinking, Job was worthy of good, not dreadful, things. At least he was worthy of fewer dreadful things than he had been getting, because even in the midst of the dreadfulness, he seemed reluctant to slander God. *That Job,* I thought. *He seems like a stand-up guy. God should be nicer; I would want an explanation too.*

I got away with thinking those things all the way to chapter 38. I even stewed about them a little. But in chapter 38, I reached the place in the book where God stops being silent. That's where my opinions and expectations started coming off their rails.

The God-speech in Job covers four chapters. It is 123 majestic and fiery verses that go on for pages. It is so intense and intimidating that midway through, Job barely dares to speak up when he's offered the chance to get a few words in edgewise.

What God says to Job, loosely paraphrased, goes something like this: *I have created everything, and I rule all. You can't create anything; you rule nothing. My creation is far bigger and grander and more complex than what you can comprehend with your puny understanding. Your questions of me are meaningless; they're as small as you are. You wouldn't want to see how things would go if it were up to you to save yourself.*

This text stunned me. I hadn't seen it coming at all. Certainly I had read Job before—at least I thought I had— and was sure I'd heard parts of it referenced in discussions and sermons over the years. In college, my Old Testament survey class had included an overview of Job, so I knew I had studied it some. But it seems I hadn't been paying attention, or maybe I hadn't read well, because my general summary of Job didn't include any kind of monumental holy scolding.

The content I remembered from Job was only this: all kinds of bad things happen unfairly to the good guy, then his three foolish friends stop by and say their long list of foolish things, then after Job endures an extended period of doubting and waiting, God makes good on the unfairness by giving Job double of all that had been taken and lost in the beginning. For his steadfast commitment, these are the kudos Job has earned. This summary of mine was a swell, misguided one, and it seems it was built less upon the premise of the book itself and more upon me. Because when I was reading Job, what I was thinking was that faith and favor should play fair.

I was thinking that all I was asking God for was one

doting man who wouldn't show up on my doorstep sloshed—easily I had done enough to deserve that. I was thinking that compared to other, less faithful women I knew who had been given good romance, surely I deserved it more. I was thinking I was spiritually and religiously entitled to universes beyond what I was actually getting. I was thinking about this huge beef I had with God for making me wait, for staying silent when I wanted to hear from him most. It wasn't body sores, livestock theft, and dead children, but it still seemed uncalled for.

God's response to Job:

> Who is this that questions my wisdom
>   with such ignorant words?
> Brace yourself like a man,
>   because I have some questions for you,
>   and you must answer them.

> Where were you when I laid the foundations
>   of the earth?
>   Tell me, if you know so much. . . .

> Can you shout to the clouds
>   and make it rain?
> Can you make lightning appear
>   and cause it to strike as you direct? . . .

> Is it your wisdom that makes the hawk soar
>   and spread its wings toward the south?
> Is it at your command that the eagle rises
>   to the heights to make its nest? . . .

Do you still want to argue with the Almighty?
You are God's critic, but do you have the answers?[4]

Um, actually, no—thanks a lot, but no, says Job. Then God speaks some more.

The true resolution in the book of Job is not the resolution I thought it would be, not the duplicate and doubled blessings raining down on faithful Job. That favor, as it turns out, is only a coda. The real resolution comes a few verses earlier, when Job, with a changed perspective, responds to God.

"I was talking about things I knew nothing about," Job says, "things far too wonderful for me. . . . I had only heard about you before, but now I have seen you with my own eyes. I take back everything I said, and I sit in dust and ashes to show my repentance."[5]

Of note: Although for thirty-seven chapters Job's innocence and deservedness have been his party line, he doesn't tout either one now. Both seem to have become irrelevant to the discussion. Job plays no more bargaining chips, and he no longer implies that life is unfair. God's greatness has silenced him and humbled him, and what he has to say is brief.

"Things I knew nothing about," Job says.

"Things," he says, "far too wonderful for me."

"But now I have seen," he says, and he shuts up entirely. It reads as something like surrender.

If in studying Job one expects the book to culminate in only reward and favor, reading it can be a frustrating experience. I disliked the idea of living in a system where I couldn't earn what I wanted from God, where even

Job-level blamelessness might not reap the rewards I was looking for. A system like that seemed too off balance and too flighty, and I was sure it would bring about only losses for me. Sudden job loss, sudden weight gain, car accidents, financial ruin, physical maiming, rejection by every man everywhere, things like that. If there was no guarantee of tangible returns on my spiritual investment, then I had lost whatever claims I might have on an eventual adoring romance and on some of the other things I wanted so badly. From my perspective, those claims were my only hope for one day getting the wanted things, since God seemed so hell-bent on not giving them to me.

As it turns out, Job 38 was a good and fitting spot for me to be. It put me in the company of somebody else who was obedient and who felt deserving of God's favor, and it showed me a God who refuses to stoop to such balance and bartering. This was a God who loves in a recklessly lopsided fashion, who mocks fairness by giving infinitely more than he gets. A God who—as I was about to see for myself—at times demands of us a fresh look.

Tremendous and
Awful News

THE CURRENT WINTER

ON MY FIRST full day living at the farm, I arrive home after
work to find seven place settings around the table, a cassoulet and vegetables coming out of the oven, and a loaf
of fresh-baked, homemade bread sliced and arranged on a
platter. When I walk through the door, one of the younger
kids yells, "She's here!" which instantly summons and gathers every other body. It is six o'clock, and people are hungry. To make it possible for all of us to eat together after
I get home from work, Kay and Matthew's family is adjust-
ing their dinner schedule; they're used to eating around five
or so.

The problem starts formulating then, about the time
I take my seat. I look around me—at the hungry kids, the

food and good bread, the clock—and the gratitude I feel is intense. It feels like a force pushing down on my shoulders, a compression all around my ribs. Day one, meal one on the farm, and all I can think about is how wonderful these people are and how much I already owe them.

After dinner, loading the dishwasher and clearing the kitchen are the only chores that need doing. Everybody helps; it takes about ten minutes. Twelve minutes, tops. When that work is done, I stand there searching for another task, preferably something meaningful and impressive. Something that might begin to compensate for the free rent and for the cassoulet, which was delicious. But the kids have already headed upstairs to finish their homework or get ready for bed. Kay has assured me the evening's household to-dos are complete; now she and Matthew have unrolled blueprints for a barn and have begun talking about fencing configurations. So after saying one more thank-you for dinner, I go downstairs to my bedroom and catch up on email. I organize the shoes in my closet. I go to bed.

Several weeks pass like that. During the day I go to work; in the evenings I eat a free meal prepared by someone else, I help committedly with dishes, then I stalk for other, bigger ways to chip in around the farm. But most of the housework either gets done during the day or is assigned to the kids in the evenings, and we haven't gotten any animals on the farm yet. There are small things I can help with, like bringing the garbage and recycling tubs back from the roadside on trash day and retrieving the mail. I eagerly fold loads of laundry forgotten in the dryer, and I make an effort to bake cookies whenever the pantry stash begins to run low. On weekends I try to make at least one meal, giving both Kay and her grocery bill a break, and I usually play games with the kids too. Still, at the end of every day, I plod down the basement stairs, feeling I'm falling short.

I find I am very much looking forward to spring, to the barn being finished. I'm looking forward to the growing things that will need tending and to the sheep and chickens that will need feeding. I'm looking forward to repaying some of the generosities I've been given, to helping and being useful. That's what I keep focusing on, and for weeks and months, that's what gets me through.

But now it is multiple homemade pasta dinners, several instances of hauling back the trash bins, and tens of dishwashing days later, and my agent and I have received a call from an editor who seems every bit as bright and wonderful as one could hope for, and she has offered us a book deal. It is tremendous and awful news.

In the time before I moved out to the farm, I often tried to picture what this moment might be like, and what I had pictured was elation. That elation always included the happy tasks of the sharing good news with family and friends, then—my preferred way of marking a great occasion—a brownie-and-fudge ice cream sundae. Everything would feel only happy and light. There would be so much happiness that it would make me consider letting the bruise on my ego fade a little. Yes, in a rush of goodwill, perhaps even that would be possible. I would stop secretly wishing that The Publisher Who Said No would one day come to regret their no sorely, that The Editor from Before would come crawling back, apologetic and pitiful. A book deal would be, I had pictured, *that* good.

But at the farm there's going to be the expanded garden. There will be fruit trees. There will be all the animals to look after and the people to care about too. There will be tilling and planting and fertilizing and weeding and picking. There will be pruning and canning. There will be feeding and watering and pen clearing and egg gathering and wool shearing. And still somebody is going to have to trek the recycling bins back from the road on Wednesdays. And I was planning to be so intricately involved in all of it. I was even working up the nerve to help de-worm the spinach leaves.

Following the publishing offer, the thought I'm having repeatedly is that in the Sunday farmhouse meeting where I talked about my work, I should've described this particular possible scenario, a book deal, more dismally. I should've told Kay and Matthew about how slowly and painstakingly I write, how unpredictably insecure I get when writing. I should've told them about the potential erratic sleep patterns, the extreme introversion, and the likelihood of my being easily annoyed and touchy. I should've made sure to say, "I will not be a dream housemate, not even close." And also, "Instead of being an asset, I will be a burden." I should have said all this loudly, many times, until I had said it enough to make them realize that living with even the ideal book deal would be a horrible idea.

They would've wisely told me, "No thanks," and I would've been out. They wouldn't have had to do anything extra on account of me. And I wouldn't have had to deal with the pressure of not helping or of free food or of falling asleep every night under the roof of somebody else's

generosity, in a bedroom painted by them in the lovely yellow-tinged color of my choosing.

The irony is not lost on me, not one bit, that while writing a book about God's grace I will every day be trying to cope with a houseful of generosities I don't deserve. And it's too late to up and move out now, because I've already committed to being a part of this place and because I assume it's impossible to write well about holy things when you're also electing for blatant hypocrisy. So it will have to be both past and present, Grace and grace. It will have to be terrible and captivating like it was the first time.

Greenlessness

THREE WINTERS AGO

ONE OF THE more often-quoted pieces of poetry in the Bible is Psalm 23, which begins like this:

> The LORD is my shepherd;
> I shall not want.
> He makes me to lie down in green pastures;
> He leads me beside the still waters.[1]

Most of us read the start of this poem and instantly picture lush, rolling, grass-covered foothills or landscapes of clover fields as far as the eye can see. The Lord is our Shepherd, and we're dreaming the ultimate sheep dream. But this is more a Midwesterner's understanding than a Middle Easterner's reality.

99

As it turns out, the hills and fields of Palestine and Israel, where this psalm and its word pictures originated, don't offer an abundance of grazing. There, pastures are chunks of desert wilderness, not meadows, and green is not exactly green.

The first time I saw an example of Israel's "green pastures," I thought somebody somewhere had gotten their wires crossed. A friend of mine had just returned from an intensive biblical history study in Palestine and Israel, and she was recounting her trip while showing me a stack of photos. While flipping through and explaining the images, she stopped at one in particular and said it showed green pastures, the same kind that make an appearance in the poetry of Psalm 23. I looked at it, looked again, and I was sure she must be mistaken. The picture seemed to be of a rock pile in close-up. There wasn't green in it anywhere.

"This is the grass," she said, and she pointed to a tuft of five or six stubby, yellowish-brown blades that were poking out almost unnoticeably from among the rocks. It was as lush as the desert wilderness gets, which is to say not lush at all.

My friend explained that in Israel, grass grows in the form of short blades along the sides of rocks, where moisture gets trapped in small bits of shade. In Israel, when grazing animals are in a green meadow, they have only enough grass to feed on for the moment. There isn't any extra. After a few bites the supply runs out. Then they're hungry and needing again, but now from their vantage point, there's not another tuft in sight. The only way for a flock of sheep in Israel to survive is to go where their shepherd leads, moment by moment, trusting for each new mouthful.[2]

The Lord is my shepherd. But there have been—there are still—times when I don't feel convinced he can be trusted for another tuft or for what seems like the right one. During the early months of the Honey Project, I had all but stopped asking God for things, even small things that had a chance of being important to me. I assumed he would rather teach me another hard lesson than dish me up some asked-for happiness or relief. I had become afraid to pray my most weighty and meaningful requests, out of fear that God might deny them instantly, for sport. When my brother David left home for Marine Corps boot camp, he had asked family and friends to pray for his safety, and I hadn't known what to do.

My only fallback plan was to keep fasting, to keep trying to be extra good. I hoped my obedience and good behavior would compel God to send me some of the favor I had been asking for. The problem with this fallback plan, however, was that it was held together by two assumptions: *I'm deserving* and *God isn't loving.* These are faulty assumptions, but I couldn't see that at the time. I also couldn't have known that both of them were about to be exploded into oblivion.

Part Three

FIG LEAF

Panties and
Other Catastrophes

THE CURRENT WINTER

ON ONE OF my first projects working at the church, it was necessary for my boss and me to collaborate with an individual from outside the church staff. This individual behaved unprofessionally. Rudely. Passive-aggressively. Sabotagingly. And she whined. It was a tense and frustrating experience, but to my thinking it went as well as could've been expected, considering that one of the parties was in the habit of throwing full-on brat tantrums.

When the project was over and we could put it on the shelf, Lee, my boss, made a point to pull me aside and tell me that my efforts had been fine and professional. He sounded apologetic, as if he might be worried I wouldn't want to stick around. Or maybe he wondered whether this was causing me to feel insecure. Either way, he said things like, "Really, the problems here had nothing to do with you," and "I know you were working as hard as you could."

It was thoughtful of Lee to say those things, and I appreciated the kindness, but for me they weren't necessary. Plus, I wanted him to know I'm generally not the kind who's looking for extra reassurance. So when I got the sense he was about to continue with more compliments, I interrupted. I interrupted my communications boss, whom I wanted to please and impress. And I interrupted him abruptly, without thinking about it much, with poor communication.

"Just so you know, typically I assume I've done everything right."

Lee's eyes widened when he heard this. Mine did too. I think we were both equally surprised at what had just been said. It's not the sort of thing one expects to hear, especially not in the presence of a boss, just down the hall from a sanctuary.

I assume I'm always right is not what I was really trying to say or what I was thinking. What I meant was that I don't often get insecure about my work. What I was thinking was, *I'm not hurt; there's no need to worry.* The problem was, however, none of that other stuff was what I actually said. What I actually said was something that sounded more like, *I find myself to be amazing.*

That story comes to mind often during my early days on the farm. I am remembering it on a regular basis, regularly recalling the conclusion I came to back then: rather than how I had intended to describe myself to Lee, how

I *did* describe myself was probably the honest way of saying the thing.

In moving into Kay and Matthew's basement, I have acquired six housemates whom I barely know: two parents and four, not five, kids. This family has built its own home life as any family does: full of routines and habits and expectations that are for the most part shared and understood by all. It flows well for them and suits them.

Kay and Matthew's family is used to certain meals, for instance, and snacks, too (all mostly organic, not a heavy showing of dairy). They have agreed-upon favorite activities (outdoor ones, usually). They've established household rules (including "Be respectful," "No sitting on kitchen counters," and "Everybody works"). These are just some of the unspoken family codes that I keep clumsily stumbling into.

First: When I move into the farmhouse, I move in some of my groceries as well. Included in the supply are four boxes of ready-to-make macaroni and cheese, complete with cartoon-shaped pasta pieces and packets of powdered cheese mix, which I happen to love and happen to eat on a somewhat regular basis. But in finding a spot for the boxes in Kay and Michael's pantry, there on a shelf beside the brown rice and organic oats and dried fruit treats, I begin to doubt my food selection. Suddenly I feel accused by the instant sauce packs, the high preservative counts, the low price tags, and the kiddy-noodle marketing schemes. I wonder if perhaps they suggest to my host family that I am immature, unrefined, unenlightened, and cheap. For a while I debate hiding the boxes in my room and making mac and cheese only when nobody else is home to see it.

Second: Not long after I move in, after being convinced

I have done a thorough check, I leave an item of underwear in the farmhouse dryer. Of all things. With children and a married man in the house. And it must be said, it is a fairly sexy piece of underwear.

I am a firm believer that both one's panties and how hidden or unhidden one keeps those panties can say a lot about the person. So when I come home from work one day to find the unmentionable piece of cotton and lace returned to me, folded neatly on the edge of my bed, I go mildly paranoid wondering what, if anything, my underwear has said. And to whom it has been speaking. I worry that I have just made myself look like some kind of hussy.

Maybe one of the boys found it, or worst of all, maybe Matthew. Maybe one of the younger kids saw fit to take it on a tour of the house, for purposes of determining ownership:

"Whose underwear is this?"

"Lemme see." (The item is held out for inspection. It is inspected.)

"I dunno."

(Next room.) "Whose underwear is this?"

"Lemme see."

Odds are, Kay is the one who found it. Odds are, she was unfazed by the finding, and there was no panty tour. Still, I blush and feel awkward during my next several conversations with every one of my new housemates, even the kids. And after every subsequent load of laundry, I now contort my neck twice—up and over to look into the barrel of the dryer, down and under for the washer—to ensure a visual all-clear of both machines. I check the nearby clothes baskets, counters, and floors with meticulous obsession.

Third: In the farmhouse basement, just down the hall
from my bedroom, there is a kitchenette with a small
refrigerator. When I move in, that fridge is playing host
to two hundred baby trees that are to be given away at an
upcoming meeting of the local arbor society chapter. Each
sapling is wrapped in its own small plastic tube, and each
plastic tube has a paper label neatly adhered around its
middle. But that fridge also has a deceptively shutting door,
as apparently it has always had. Even when it looks closed,
you have to finish the job with a sealing shove. I don't
know this yet.

One evening after picking up a few groceries, I put a
bottle of orange juice in the door of the fridge, and afterward I do not shove. Instead I go about my evening, and
I head to bed. When I wake up in the morning, the freezer
portion of the mini-fridge has defrosted and dripped melt-
ing ice over all the tree tubes and all their labels. Inside the
clear plastic cylinders there are droplets everywhere, some
forming tiny streams, and on the outside the paper has
turned wrinkled and mushy. Water is all over the floor—
so much that it requires my entire supply of bath towels
to sop it up, plus a couple of beach towels too. I try for a
few minutes to give the tree tubes some hope of being neat
and presentable again, but it becomes quickly clear there's
no use. Before leaving for work, I find Kay and break
the news.

Later that day, on the phone with a friend, I recount
with chagrin the story of the fridge door and the drippy,
lumpy-labeled sapling tubes. What I say at the end of the
story is, "Well, at least we know that they know I'm not
perfect." I say this with a partial laugh, which makes light

of the point, and with blushing, which doesn't. It is low-grade blushing, but still.

In the life of someone less inclined to be high strung and twitchy, trivial events like these would likely be unaffecting, barely worth a mention. But here I am mentioning them, because these trivial events rock me with uncertainty. They grate on me. They leave me feeling agitated and ashamed, tense and precarious. This does not bode well for me, because as time passes on the farm, the saplings and the panties and the macaroni incidents turn out to be just a preamble.

Several months pass on the farm; during that time I spend weeknight hours and most weekends in my basement bedroom, attempting to type sentences and paragraphs that are meaningful enough to make a manuscript. It is strained. It is laborious. It is not fruitful or promising.

This is writer's block on speed: I have one document for sections that are potentially decent or salvageable, another document for the pages that must never see the light of day ever. The "keep" pieces are one-quarter as long as they should be by now, which is terrifying to me, and they are outnumbered ten to one by the junk. I am not being modest in saying that. There is a vast abundance of garbage, and at this rate I'm worried I won't be able to produce even a bad first draft on deadline. Some days it feels like panic. I begin to feel utterly dependent on a miracle or a cosmic breakthrough. I am every day dreading the moment when my editor will have to witness the mess.

Almost daily and sometimes more often than that, Kay or Matthew or one of their kids asks me how the writing is going. I am optimistic and tell them that either "It's going all right" or "It's just okay today." Then I smile or shrug, and if there's a pause in the conversation, I try to change the subject. I am unaware that this is my pattern until one day in the kitchen when, having been asked the writing question by Kay, I tell her it's going incredibly today and that I am amazed.

"Yay!" she says. She nearly jumps in the air, then she hugs me. "It's so rare to hear that!" she says.

What I haven't realized until that moment is, it's rare to think it too. I am hanging on by threads. I am working as hard as I possibly can, and the primary result seems to be only my complete inability to get things right. Most of my efforts are turning out wrong.

The failure is as startling and humbling as ever—this, despite the fact that with my past experiences in the world of grace, I should easily know to expect it.

Gut Reactions

THREE WINTERS AGO

ON THE FIRST day of my sweets fast there were five caramel cubes, four Tootsie Rolls, and two pink Starbursts in
a candy dish at the reception area down the hall from my
office. I filled most of my working hours trying to not
think about them. Several times while walking past, I used
all my willpower to avoid looking at them. For the duration of two meetings I daydreamed about them. After that,
I went back to my computer, and with a cursor blinking
faithfully in front of me, I tried to focus on work. But the
nearness of the sweets put all the words and sentences in
a jumble.

For breakfast that day I had eaten toast with peanut
butter; what I had wanted, painfully wanted, was a frosted

cinnamon roll from the bakery down the street. Lunch
had been reheated pasta with water to drink. The water
had been nothing new—it had been my beverage of choice
for at least a year, maybe two, by then. But as I drank it, I
found that fasting had already made me fickle: the break-
room fridge was stocked with a few rows of sodas that were
up for grabs, and I had become irrationally grouchy about
not being able to sip one between bites of bow-tie Alfredo.

By this time I had begun making my first two fasting
observations:

Observation 1: Self-discipline is not for the faint of
heart.

Observation 2: I think I might be the faint of heart.

The night before that first day of the fast, it had seemed
iffy at best that I'd have the strength to go through with
the fast. That night I spent an hour or two in my kitchen,
purging sweets from my pantry, refrigerator, and freezer,
then from my purse, desk, bedside table, and glove compartment. It felt relentless. By the end of the purification,
both my garbage can and recycling tub were overflowing.
Their contents: half-eaten bags of cookies, several mini-
tubs of Ben & Jerry's, three bottles of non-fruit fruit juice,
most of my cereals, an almost-new package of red licorice,
and from the back of my go-to snack cabinet, handfuls of
fun-size Snickers and Milky Ways. The quantity of sweets
was disarming, and it made me wonder if perhaps I had
a bigger sweet tooth than I'd realized. How many pints of
candy-swirled ice cream does one person need?

After a quick trip to the garbage cans outside, I walked
back into my apartment and stood just within the doorway for a while. This was when the fast seemed newly

real. I didn't know what to think or how to plan. I tried to come up with a surefire procedure for getting through the first craving. I gave myself a pep talk about saying no to processed sugar, about the goodness of having fruits and fruit juices and honey instead. But all that time, really I was thinking about how much I loved my favorite treats, about how much—this sounds pitiful, I know—I would miss them. I was thinking about restocking my pantry with Nutty Bars. And the question I kept asking myself was, *How will I survive this?* The answer seemed clear by the next day, mid-morning, about an hour after the caramel cubes, the Starbursts, and the Tootsie Rolls took over my thoughts: I wouldn't.

Someone once told me that the point of fasting is to remind us that we are weak. Point taken. I had had no idea, before the Honey Project began, just how much my life was bossed by sweets. Fasting, in a matter of just hours, seemed to have overturned and overruled the whole scope of my senses. There is no excuse for a grown woman to spend the majority of a day thinking about sugar, but for the whole of that first day, I wasn't able to make myself stop. And there was a taste of bitter blandness in my mouth, constant since before I'd gotten out of bed. My taste buds were in revolt. A few hours later, I was feeling irritable and lethargic, drained of energy, but with an appetite that wouldn't quit.

Surely all those effects couldn't be directly tied to the fast. Could they? The thought seemed ridiculous. But with every sweet-free minute that wore on, I felt more and more certain about the connection. After work that first day I went home and opened and closed and reopened my kitchen cupboards endlessly. Later that evening I turned on the TV and tried to erase the mental images of all the sweets I couldn't eat in that moment. After a couple of sit-com episodes I gave up and plodded off to bed. It wasn't wholly implausible, I began to think, that at the tail end of the fast I'd be sitting on the floor in a dark corner some-where, either foaming at the mouth or clinically depressed.

Another sweets-free morning broke. And another. And another. As the fasting days on my calendar marched on, things got worse before it appeared there might be a chance they'd get better. By this I mean that one night I found a couple of homemade brownies in the freezer; I must have missed them in the all-sweets apartment purification spree. To keep from eating them I had to throw them into the garbage and then coat them with liquid dish soap. It was disconcerting, to have stooped to that.

On another day, home in my apartment, frustrated and distracted by all that was lacking in my kitchen, I decided I needed to get away. I left home suddenly, and in the pro-cess I also left my circa-1962 oven on and unattended for seven hours.

One night I wrote about cravings in my journal. I quote: "An Almond Joy commercial nearly ruined me today."

Several weeks in, my boss brought a couple dozen pas-tries to work with her. I peered inside the box just long enough to see a doughnut with chocolate frosting and sprinkles, my favorite. I wanted it so badly I thought my intestines were going to implode.

All these reactions to fasting felt embarrassingly exces-sive to me, but for weeks, maybe months, it seemed impos-sible to contain them. On regular occasions I had to make concentrated efforts to decipher real logic from cravings.

Partly this was due to the fact that the entire cavity of my mouth had started tasting like two-day-old garlic. (Was it theatrical to dwell on a thought like that? Was I imagining things, exaggerating for the sake of flair? But then I would swallow to assess the flavor. The taste was thick and awful, and no one could've made it up.) Sweetness was the one thing that could cleanse my palate—I was sure it would do the trick, but sweetness was precisely what I had vowed not to have. Each time there was an occasion for a meal or for a snack or a drink, none of the options in sight would satisfy. Most days there was only this one drumming repetition: what I wanted was chocolate, chocolate. The true low point was when I practically leered at a Hershey's bar.

Occasionally I would think about these cravings and what they pointed to. I would think about, as my friend Drew calls it, the "realer still," and I would try to figure out what the Honey Project was teaching me. I would try to guess at whether it would amount to much of anything beyond insane levels of hunger and sweets longing.

What I didn't know at that time was this: part of what's so incredible about fasting and other spiritual disciplines is the way they put physicality on faith. They tie our understanding of God to everyday tangibility, creating a connection between bodily habit—eating, perhaps—and soul. Between, for instance, the taste of that Twinkie in the cupboard and the reality of divine sweetness. Thus, spiritual disciplines help turn belief into something that can literally stare us in the face. We'll never look at prepackaged snack cakes the same way again.

Smartly

THREE WINTERS AGO

NOT MORE THAN a few weeks into the Honey Project, I had
started thinking about debt. This was the natural, though
unanticipated, result of my being a few thousand dollars
in debt.

At the time my financial MO had seemed harmless to
me, even healthy: each month I paid my bills, including the
minimum amount due on my credit card, then I bought
myself things. The week before my sweets fast began, for
instance, while staring down the barrel of a thousands-large
Visa bill, I made up my mind to go on a cruise. This decision had been foolish for the obvious fiscal reasons and also
because I sunburn easily. But when I looked into the trip,
the ticket price was on discount, the Michigan snow was

piling up, and Cora (who lived within driving distance of the port city) was free to be my cabin mate. Besides, I had picked up a stock of vacation days in the new year.

I figured: perpetual reapplication of sunscreen. I figured: what's another few hundred bucks on credit?

For a while I allowed myself to be pleased about this witless expense, but several weeks later my Visa bill arrived, and the mushrooming "Amount Due" at the top of the page twisted knots in my stomach. I couldn't believe I'd let myself rack up so much debt. How many months (years?) would it take, on my not-for-profit ghostwriter's salary, to pay off a total like that? How in the world had I managed to completely avoid such a question before? So that night, with trepidation, I forced myself to sit down with a calculator, the bill, and over a year's worth of bank statements to sort things out and take a total inventory. The process was ugly, and the math was too. But it gave me some workable answers, which was more than I'd had when I started.

The answer to the first how, the how about a payoff timeline, had a range of options depending on my diligence—I'm something of a details geek, so yes, I took the time to calculate this. The best-speed scenario would take no less than fifteen months, which sounded nice on paper but in reality was not uplifting. If I wanted to make it happen, I would have to increase my monthly bill payment by something like 400 percent, and the only way to do that would be to become continually, dismally frugal. To wit, at least fifteen months of buying practically nothing. I checked and rechecked those numbers for half an hour, hoping they were wrong. They weren't.

In an attempt to console myself about this, I figured

out some budgets for more leisurely payoff scenarios. They
allowed for some spending, so at a glance they had seemed
less terrifying. But I hadn't forgotten eighth-grade algebra
completely, and I knew that the more prolonged schedule
would mean more interest accrued in the long run. There
was, I could see now, no pleasant route back to an even zero.
This news was horrible. It made me want to go shopping.

But. There would be no more staying financially stupid,
I decided. Good judgment was long overdue, and some
changes were necessary. That night I made up my mind that
I would make the debt payoff my first financial priority.
I wouldn't spend money on something, on *anything*, unless
spending money was absolutely unavoidable. It wasn't until
after I had made up my mind and committed to this that
I had remembered there was a cruise on my calendar.

My shoulders slumped. It felt like the second hard hit
of a one-two punch. Since booking the Caribbean vacation,
not only had I adopted a fast from sweets—read: automatic
pass on Thursday's all-night, all-dessert buffet at sea—but
now I was also going to have to spend minuscule amounts
of money, zero if possible, in an environment where people
were shelling out eighteen dollars for every margarita. And
how was I supposed to do that quietly, without having to
admit to Cora the reasons behind my zero cruise purchases?
Knowing Cora, if I told her about my massive deficit, she
would be generous and offer to buy things for me, which
would probably make me feel guiltier. As if all that weren't
enough, putting myself on a budget in advance of the trip
meant I wouldn't be able to buy any cruising clothes to be
breezy and tropical.

But of all the places where a budget can maintain a

low profile (at least after the initial, nonrefundable fee), it had seemed that a most-expenses-included sail was probably one of the best. So I went, I applied sunscreen, and I almost completely didn't spend. My only purchases were a couple of trinkets I bought when I was with Cora, to keep her off my tracks. I had taken fifty dollars in cash with me, and on the last day I had thirty-eight dollars left. I was doing just fine.

As is customary on some cruises, all passengers were required to tip the service staff at the end of the trip. We were given the option of paying by cash or credit card. When I went to the porter's desk to reconcile my tip fee, I was thinking about which I should choose. I knew Cora was planning to drop me off at the airport on her drive home from the dock, and since I would be in airports from then on for the rest of the day, I figured I could use my credit card for any emergencies that might pop up in those places. As a way of adding as little as possible to the balance on my credit card, I gave the porter all my cash and then charged just a few dollars to cover the remaining portion of tips. Leaving the ship just a few minutes later, I was smiling with satisfaction: I had managed my money so smartly.

But as Cora and I made our way to the parking garage, she made a suggestion.

"You know," Cora said, "there are all kinds of airport shuttles over there. I bet it would be quicker and easier for you to catch a ride with one of them."

I looked. Sure enough, there were shuttles.

"It would save me some time on my trip home," Cora added. "And I bet they're probably free."

I started getting nervous. For a split second I thought,

Tell her you spent your cash. That's all you have to say. Ask if she can float you a twenty, just in case. But I didn't want to embarrass myself.

"Sure," I said, "that's probably a good idea."

We were about fifty yards from the vans. As I said good-bye to Cora and toted my suitcases toward them, I felt my throat clenching. I prayed over and over that the shuttle ride would be Visa-friendly. I reminded God that after my first dinner on the boat I had passed over the cheesecake dessert option and had selected the fruit plate. I asked him to throw me a bone.

At the first van with empty space in it, I handed my suitcase to somebody at the back of the vehicle, then climbed inside and took a seat in the second row. Directly in front of me, taped to the back of the driver's seat, was a simple printout:

Airport shuttle $5/person

Cash or check **ONLY!!**

My stomach started twisting all over itself.

People were filling up the seats beside me—there was no easy way out, plus my luggage was at the bottom of the pile in the back. I had no cash. I had no checks. I was sure Cora was already to her car by then, and how could I ask her to come back? How would I explain myself? By the time the driver loaded up all the bags, shut the doors, and took his place up front, I still hadn't figured out a way to get out of this. My hands started shaking.

"Sir? Sir?" It was the only option I had left.

The driver turned around. He did not appear to be overly kindhearted.

I stammered. I was at the edge of tears. "I'm . . . I'm sorry, but . . . but—"

The whole vanload of people was staring at me. Terrible, terrible.

"—all I have . . . is . . . a credit card. Is that . . . okay?"

He didn't even pause. He narrowed his eyes, raised both eyebrows, and pointed to the sign on the back of his seat. "It's cash or check," he emphasized, "*only*." As if to match the sign itself, his *only* sounded bold, all caps, and double-underlined.

The air that had been momentarily constrained in my lungs gusted out, and with that one exhale I started loudly and messily and helplessly crying, there in the second seat of the shuttle. Then several things happened all at once. The driver made a face of disgust. The passengers next to me looked out the window nervously, as if hoping this whole scenario would go away. Somebody whispered in the backseat.

Also in the van, however, in the first bench seat, a pair of petite, almost-old ladies had a different reaction. They turned toward me, grabbing feverishly at their purses and pulling out their wallets. Then, before I fully realized what was happening, both of them pushed a five-dollar bill into my hands.

"Here, honey. You just take it."

"Sweetie, here you go."

My thoughts were spinning, and my hands were

gripping the money. Tears were blurring my vision. I felt foolish and lost and small.

As quickly as they had turned toward me, the Petites turned toward the front again and briskly started a conversation. They seemed embarrassed, and I couldn't tell whether they felt the emotion for themselves or for me. The shuttle driver turned to the front too, shaking his head, starting the engine, and pulling away from the curb. Others began shifting and settling into their seats. In no time, things came to appear almost as if nothing out of the ordinary had happened. But I was sitting there stunned and hiccup-crying, holding cash that wasn't mine and was more than I needed.

On instinct I reached forward with the extra five-dollar bill and held it out in front of the petite ladies. I thanked them, then I somewhat-hiccuppingly urged them to take back the second five. I had my credit card, I told them, and I didn't need anything more than the shuttle fare.

"No, no, just take it," said Petite One.

"Really, no," said Two.

To say this, they only partway turned toward me, and for only a moment, then they continued their conversation.

Everything in me wanted to find a way to fix this, to justify myself. But the moment felt beyond repair. There was no way to prove to these people that I wasn't the kind of unprepared, overemotional, scrounging wreck of a person I appeared to be. So for a while I stayed perched on the edge of my seat, voiceless and defeated. Even my crying had been stunned to a stop. Then I scooted back and hunched against the window.

When we got to the airport, I thanked the two ladies

once more, but with only a nod and a half-smile. I was still holding both of their five-dollar bills, crumpled in one hand. I waited on the curb while the driver unloaded luggage and passengers toted their suitcases away. My bag was the last to come out of the van; I grabbed it from the driver before it could touch the ground. I handed him one of the Petite's fives, without words and without eye contact. Then I ducked my head and hurried away, shoving the other Petite's bill deep in the pocket of my jeans as I went. I wanted to forget about it as quickly as possible.

But late that evening, back at my apartment after a couple of flights and a long layover, I began emptying my pockets and pulled out the five. When I realized what I was holding, I immediately dropped the bill onto the nearest surface, which happened to be my kitchen table. Just a five-dollar bill, but I tensed up and took several steps away, as if afraid of being bitten. For a long time I stood there, eyeing it warily.

The incident on the van with the petite ladies, the ten dollars, and the other shuttling cruisers wasn't just a blip on the grace radar. It turns out it was simply an indication that a stopped-up dam was ready to burst. This was just the first plug popping loose.

Waiting: Woe Poker

THREE WINTERS AGO

MY FRIEND SHAWNA was wanting to have a baby. She was
thirty-two. She had been married, blissfully, for less than
a year. She was not pregnant.

Soon after my cruise, Shawna and I met for an
impromptu dinner at IHOP and had a long conversation about all things womb related. Over the course of the
meal I had two prevailing thoughts. First: when trying to
rid one's diet of processed sugar, the ideal location for dinner is not a place that specializes in blueberry short stacks
and five flavors of syrup. Second: this pregnancy talk is
annoying.

I was tired. I was bored with my job and ornery about
most of my life. It had been an awful day. I wanted syrup.

So when Shawna somewhat angrily told me that she was afraid God would never give her children—she confided that she practically *knew* he would deny her that dream—I confess I didn't have much sympathy for her, and I didn't want to either. I further confess that I was yelling at her in my head.

Shawna's face strained with emotion, her eyes brimmed with tears, and she spoke heartbroken words tinged with longing. Yet as I sat across the booth from her and her plate of strawberry crepes, I listened to her claims of pain and sorrow only well enough to rank them. What I was doing was playing a silent game of Woe Poker: with every sadness Shawna put in play, I mentally outbid it before that chip had even been slid to the center of the table.

I see your eight months of trying. I have friends who can raise you: two decades.

The comparison that came to mind was Cora and Jack, who had begun praying to become parents just a few years after their wedding and who at the nearly twenty-year mark of their marriage were still childless. I had met them sometime around anniversary number fifteen, which happened to also be the year that an emergency hysterectomy for Cora had officially ended any possibility of a pregnancy.

Cora and Jack are two studied, sensible, critically thinking, culturally aware people, and theirs is no flighty, glass-naively-full faith. "We believed that God would give us a child if he wanted to," Cora told me once, and what amazed me about that statement was the simplicity and clarity with which she had said it, like the belief went all the way to the core. They had asked God and they had trusted and then they had waited. Twenty years later, their

story was one of pregnancies that hadn't carried to term
and others that simply hadn't happened, not to mention
adoption possibilities that never materialized.

The longing Cora felt over this was deep and striking.
She didn't understand why God's answer had been no and
no and continually no, and there were still times when the
loss she felt was written over every angle of her face. She
wasn't angry or bitter. She wasn't even asking for a baby
anymore. She was just tired.

So in the grand scheme of Woe, as I listened (albeit
unenthusiastically) to Shawna's story of hurt, confusion,
and yearning for motherhood, what stuck out to me was
her lack of tiredness. That distinction irritated me beginning the moment I became aware of it; from there it
seemed that the more I heard the harsher I got until finally
I worked myself into a real snit. By the time we left the restaurant, I had spent about thirty minutes mentally telling
Shawna off. Her thirtysomething IHOP edition of baby-
wanting seemed mostly rosy, I kept wanting to point out,
when it was lit by a postsurgical, postmenopausal version.
Newsflash to the newlywed: you are having sex all the time,
and you still have a uterus.

But I kept my mouth shut long enough to get in my
car and drive home. This decision was noble by only a
fraction. I had some level of awareness, yes, that being
judgmental and harsh in a situation like this wasn't the
response that was called for by a friend. Also, Shawna was
a good friend who was having a bad night and who was
saying the kinds of things people say when they're caught
up and fearful. Who could blame her? The main reason
I hadn't let loose with my comments, though, was that

I couldn't figure out a way to be biting and cruel without looking like a royal jerk.

What I had wanted to somewhat forcefully suggest to Shawna was that if our roles were reversed and she were made to sit in my place at the IHOP booth, she might think it was I who had more reasons to be dissatisfied. Specifically, I had wanted to remind her that in her own former days as a single woman, even she had found it ridiculous when young wives complained to her that they were unhappy. Yet there she was, making a fuss about how her repeated conjugal romps with her adoring husband hadn't yet produced a pregnancy. It seemed she had somehow become blithely ignorant of the notion that some women, baby or not, would be elated just to have a husband to romp with.

I was alone in the car when I thought all this; nonetheless I pinched the unringed skin on my ring finger for added sass and emphasis.

And furthermore! Some women hadn't gotten a word in edgewise all night, and now we were going home to an empty apartment without anybody there to talk to and without any consoling ice cream in the freezer.

And! Some of us, in the broader category of birds and bees, seemed to be stalled and sputtering far earlier in the game than at the question of reproduction.

Not to mention! Some of us had been seated across from a friend for the long duration of a meal, and the whole time that friend hadn't once, not once, asked us about our crummy day.

For a while I let myself sulk about this; it brought me a certain level of satisfaction. I thought back to the way

Shawna's fork had dug into the whipped topping on one of her crepes, and I remembered how drab my buttered whole-wheat toast had seemed on the same table. Having compared the two, I felt in a way superior. *I see your infertility; I raise you: virginity.*

Shrink

THREE WINTERS AGO

A FEW DAYS after the IHOP incident I called a counselor's office to request an appointment with one of the psychologists. The lady who answered the phone told me that in order to qualify for co-pays, I would need to contact my health insurance provider and express that I had been feeling some anxiety or depression. Before then I wouldn't have thought to label it as either of those things; it was more like I had been chugging too many bad emotional cocktails and was starting to feel the first pangs of a hangover. So I called the insurance company and said it was anxiety, probably, and I booked an hour-long appointment with Dr. P— for a week out. Then I began prepping for the session by taking mental notes of my most obvious problems. Such as:

On day three, my friend Annie told me that she saw Urban Cole out for coffee with another girl. Annie was apologetic to tell me this. "But I knew you'd want to know," she said. I didn't let her see how much it bothered me to hear the news, but I went home and felt like something vital had collapsed, maybe somewhere near my rib cage. I regretted telling her, regretted telling anyone, about my feelings for UC, because now it was turning into another public nothing. And I felt sad—a weird, deep, self-doubt kind of sad—and I let myself assume for no reason whatsoever that no man would ever notice me. Then in an unexpected mental joggle, suddenly I was strategizing for summer's upcoming wedding receptions. If I stood alone during the dancing, I thought, and held eye contact with guys around the room, maybe it would work in my favor for a handsome partner on some of the slow songs.

Day four, I tried to talk my sister out of planning a desserts-only wedding reception. This had little to do with my fast from sweets; I was annoyed thinking that she would host an evening wedding and not offer the guests a real meal. When our mom stepped in to suggest I was overreacting and maybe a little too attached to the bridal menu, I told her *I am not*, then spent the next half hour either sobbing or post-sob whimpering.

Day six, I bought a party dress and two new sweaters online. I was unable to think of a single occasion when I would have a reason to wear the dress, and the sweaters were wildly overpriced, but I wanted so badly to feel beautiful and have all three. An hour after making the purchases, my mental haze cleared enough for me to remember I was already almost three grand in debt to Visa. I felt stupid and shallow then, and I knew I'd have to return the whole order.

Day eight, I returned the clothes. I felt slightly better after that, even though I had already charged my credit card, and there would be no refund on the fee for shipping.

Days three, five, and nine, I cried at peculiar intervals about my job, about family moving away, about my little brother getting ready for boot camp, about not spending my money wisely, about dessert receptions, about UC, about crying so much, about losing track of my own life. Days one, two, and seven weren't so bad.

Having amassed this list of topics well before my first appointment with Dr. P——, I went to his office on the day of the session and felt confident that at least there wouldn't be any awkward silences. I quickly discovered, however, that keeping up the chatter was hardly something I needed to concern myself with.

He asked just one question, and a benign one at that: "What would you like to talk about today?"

I don't know what caused what came next, whether it was the cliché-turned-reality of sitting on a psychologist's couch or whether it was my sugar deficiency making itself known or whether it was just how my nerves spiked slightly when I looked at the manila folder and the note paper in Dr. P——'s hands. In answering him, I not only went twenty minutes over the allotted one-hour time frame, but within the first five of those minutes I had already tossed most of my conversation starters out the window. I barely thought about what to say; I just spoke. What came out was a tangled mess of words and probably a fair bit of senselessness thrown in too.

I told him stories about my relationship with my sister, going as far back as elementary school to recall the long line of young men who had been fascinated by Sarah and disinterested in me. I speculated as to why, telling him that she was blonde and that she had always been thinner and more admiring. I told him about all the upcoming weddings and how much I was dreading hers. I told him how afraid I was that my envy would ruin the day not just for me but for other people, too, and most of all for Sarah. I told him I was twenty-four years old, and since fifth grade no guy had liked me enough to do anything about it.

I debated stopping at that—it was certainly enough to work with—but I went on, admitting to Dr. P— that flirting was a mystery to me and that as much as I tried I couldn't figure out how to interact with single men in ways that seemed normal. I told him that everything I did felt like *trying* and that I hated it. *Trying* to become more interesting, *trying* to be attractive and approachable, *trying* to become someone different from who I had always been, because who I had always been obviously wasn't working. I told him I wanted to trust that God could bring somebody incredible into my life—to sit back and really *trust*—but that instead I was always and only trying. When I was done telling him all these things, I stopped and felt suddenly embarrassed. It wasn't until the retrospect that came much later that I realized the story had come out half-digested, like psych puke all over Dr. P—'s shiny dress shoes.

He calmly glanced at a clock and said our time was almost up. (Bless him, our time had been almost up a full fifteen minutes earlier.) He told me that before I left, there was one thing he wanted to know. The big question,

Dr. P— said, was: Could I explain the difference between trying and trusting? How did I know when I was trying and when I wasn't? What would be different about my life if I started trusting?

They seemed like the sort of questions that begged quickly evident answers, like I should've had no problem firing off an astute response from my place on the couch. Instead, I sat there mutely, and I took up another full minute of my already extended time by looking out the window. I felt stupefied about myself and guilty for having stayed so long. My eyes were stinging and squinty, both from the brightness of the sun and from all the crying.

I told Dr. P— I didn't have a good answer. He nodded, then told me my assignment for the next few weeks was to see if I could come up with one.

Rude, Nude

THREE WINTERS AGO

HERE IS AN attempt at a good answer. At the start of Genesis 3, Adam and Eve eat fruit from the tree of the knowledge of good and evil, which is the only tree God had forbidden them to eat from. As a result, a cosmic chasm opens between them and their Creator. The rest of the chapter recounts Adam and Eve running naked and shamefaced through a garden, tattling on each other, grabbing fig leaves to keep everything PG, and lying to God. When God shows up in the Garden for a walk and asks them what they're up to, they point out the obvious, which is that they're naked. They tell him they heard him coming and felt ashamed.

A while ago I heard a recording of a sermon by Timothy

Keller, one of my favorite preachers and Bible scholars, built around this passage.[1] Keller notes in the sermon that Adam and Eve's self-proclaimed problem of nakedness obviously wasn't their real problem. It couldn't have been, he points out, because nakedness wasn't the thing that had changed. Adam and Eve had always been naked. In the very beginning, when everything was very good, they were fully exposed before each other and before God, all the time. That, Keller says, was what had been so good about it.

The word *naked* was originally understood to mean "known." Keller says that in the beginning Adam and Eve had no fear of being known or revealed—not to themselves, not to each other, not to God. Everything felt worthy of being known, so honesty with others felt okay. But in becoming people whose actions no longer matched God's desires for them, Adam and Eve became afraid of being fully seen. They became vulnerable; they didn't want to be known for what they really were, and their first inclination was to take cover. Suddenly the idea of total exposure to God and to anyone else seemed unthinkable.

Sin was the problem, and feeling exposed was the first symptom. This is a common order of things.

Before the Honey Project, I was really good at not thinking about my sin. I didn't even have to try to not think about it; not thinking about it was my automatic inclination. I obeyed God's commandments and with gusto. I was involved in church. I memorized Bible verses. I tried not to gossip or lie much. I didn't say *heck*. I didn't wear bikinis or short shorts. I built formulaic spreadsheets for my budget in order to ensure a 10 percent minimum tithe on my income, even in a few instances when IOUs were necessary. Sin? Who had time to think about sin?

Back then I thought a life in Christ was about elegance and polish. I thought betterment was the only objective: refine yourself with good behavior, and then you'll know your faith is true. As far as I knew, that was the litmus for determining a true Christian life, and to my thinking, it was reliable like a petri dish experiment. Q: Is she a Christian? A: Is there mold on the gel? And it seemed obvious there always had been.

Then I began fasting from sweets, and suddenly I started having trouble being good. I started having a lot of trouble being good. Wherever I turned, I was making mistakes, hurting people, being misunderstood, and making a mess of things. This didn't make sense, because I was still trying to behave in the same careful way I had always behaved.

I overdrafted my bank account six times. I forgot to pay my rent. A guy I knew pulled me aside one day and not-so-vaguely implied he thought I had a pride issue. I unintentionally broke my word to two friends, risking a permanent rift with them. In a counseling session with Dr. P—, after I talked with him for a while about faith, he became visibly frustrated and told me I was self-righteous. He told me that even my posture was self-righteous, which made me think there must've been truth in the claim; otherwise he wouldn't have been so undone and over the top about it.

One day a man I'll call Doug introduced himself via an awkward cold-call email; in about ten sentences he mentioned that he knew some distant relatives of mine, told me his age, listed his recent volunteer roles and places of occupation, stated that he was looking for a godly woman to share his life with, and asked me if I would be willing to meet for coffee. It read like a mechanical, slapdash dating résumé. After reading it, I took almost no time in sending my blunt response, which went something like: Thank you, Doug, but no, I am not interested in being your godly wife. He replied that he found me rude and heartless, which I probably was. Little did he know, I was also increasingly jealous of every married woman everywhere, not to mention spittingly annoyed by the engaged ones. Plus I wanted candy more than ever.

It was humiliating to fail and fall short in ways like these. It was perplexing, too, I will admit, because my crop of blunders seemed so bodily and base. I figured I should be above screwing up in such common categories. Still, I couldn't find a way to reverse the breakdown. No matter how hard I kept trying to be good, I kept making more and bigger and uglier mistakes.

Fasting brought out a brand-new mirror, I found. It was embarrassing to face my reflection in it, complete with sins I was incapable of ridding myself of, not even in tiny or simple ways. This, for someone who lived life thinking she was very good, was a major blow. It was like standing there naked, under bad lighting—I had never felt so exposed. Without sweets, my flaws and my spiritual flab and all my inadequacies were bared, and I couldn't find a fig leaf anywhere that would be big enough to cover who I was.

The Farm Ladies

THE CURRENT WINTER

EARLY ONE EVENING late in the fall, our flock of sheep arrives on the farm. There are six of them, all ewes; we have decided to call them The Ladies and give them names like Phyllis, Dolly, Heldred, and Lady Lou. My first in-person impression of the ewes, however, is that they are quite unladylike and that they are truly stupid.

Their first notable trait is that they seem always afraid. When they're afraid and confined to the back of a transport truck, two things happen: they lock their legs so as to become immobile, and their excretory systems kick into overdrive. Matthew tells us they were afraid and jittery on their short drive to the farm. This is not surprising, because even a slight sudden movement within a thirty-foot radius scares them all stiff. Then when I first meet the sheep, they can't seem to decide which is more terrifying: jumping out of the truck, staying in it, or tracking every movement of every person who gets close to them. It makes for a less than grand arrival, to be sure. By the time all six of them are coaxed or pulled into pasture, the entire floor of the truck bed is smeared with turds and urine.

It takes little time to see that when The Ladies are afraid and *not* confined to a small space, their response is the expected excrement as well as constant skittishness and running. For the first several weeks, the sheep are jumping away and bolting off almost any time a person is in sight. Even when that person is Matthew, their caretaker, and even when he is clearly carrying food or vitamins. They run and kick over their water bucket. They run into the electric fence and get the shock that's intended for the coyotes. Or they run over and out of that fence, escaping the safety of their paddock. In this version, the minute they're on the other side, separated from the rest of The Ladies by that thin grid of wires, they lose it. Now afraid of jumping back over the fence, they run to try to find a break in it. Then they run away from Matthew, who is opening the fence and trying to corral them back in.

On many levels the cluelessness of these sheep is hilarious. I stand out in the field or at my bedroom window, watching and rolling my eyes and giggling as they war against themselves. When rubber boots and ewe chasing are necessary, I play my part in the chase, then I laugh all the way back to the farmhouse.

But. And.

In the Bible, sheep are a choice metaphor for God's

people; it is an image that appears in the Psalms, in the Prophets, in the parables of Jesus, in the letters of Paul, and in other epistles. Apparently this must be something to be taken seriously. It must also mean that looking at six ewes in a pasture is seeing ourselves, is seeing me. Which, if I force myself to make honest comparisons, isn't quite the stretch I'd like it to be.

My preference—and my default mode—is to go on believing I am mostly good, just occasionally misguided. It is soothing to me, this illusion that I am not small and insignificant . . . that I am not undisciplined and unprincipled . . . that I am not the sort who fails to follow through on her promises . . . that the core of my character is not at all ugly or awkward or unseemly . . . that I am less sinful, not more, than I think I am. Or at least that I am equally the person I think I am.

But here I am, having sought out and accepted far too many responsibilities for one person to handle responsibly. Here I am, somehow expecting to accomplish them all. Here I am, having juggled friendships poorly, having offered only abrupt cutoffs or constant apologies when life got busy. Here I am, attempting those relationships plus a community's worth of brand-new ones too. Here I am, making promises and not knowing how to keep them. Here I am, uncovered and unpresentable, with all kinds of flaws being nakedly exposed. Here I am, being foolish and truly stupid.

I am learning one lesson though, however slowly. What I am learning is to remember that this endless fallenness is a most necessary part of faith. In that way, it has a sort of silver lining: the sharp, crude exposure of sin is a setup to the rest of the story.

Part Four

CHEAP SWEET COUNTERFEIT

Silent-Competitive Preaching

THE CURRENT SPRING

A FEW MONTHS AGO I heard a sermon about Abraham; it
was one of those great sermons where the preacher includes
little-known facts and figures about the original setting
of the featured biblical text in order to help illumine its
meaning. I'm assuming, at least, that the sermon turned
out to be a great one. I got sidetracked by the trivia halfway
through and never came back mentally.

Part of the problem for me was that going into the
sermon, I already felt largely familiar with the story of
Abraham: This was the guy who starts out in one land
with one name, Abram; then God calls him away from
that land, telling him to go to a different one. Abram goes,
and when he arrives at the new land, God promises to give

it to Abram's children. Except that Abram and his wife, Sarai, don't have any children. Decades pass; all kinds of things happen (God changes Abram's name to Abraham, Abraham impregnates a servant, Abraham almost sells his wife to a king, God destroys two cities, Abraham's niece-in-law is turned to salt, etc., etc.), yet no children are born to Abraham and his wife.

At the respective ages of one hundred and ninety, Abraham and Sarah (her name changed too) have a child, a boy, and name him Isaac. Not too long after that, however, God tells Abraham to walk Isaac up a mountain and sacrifice him, a command to which there's no good response, when you think about it. But Abraham goes. He and his son walk up the mountain, and Abraham straps that promised child on an altar and even raises his knife in the air before God intervenes. He shows Abraham a ram that's stuck in some brush and tells him to sacrifice the animal instead. Then God promises to bless Abraham greatly since he was willing to give up his only son. He tells Abraham that his children will be numerous like stars in the sky and grains of sand on the beach.

That's the gist of it, familiar as anything.

The piece of trivia that threw me off the sermon trail had to do with the beginning of the story. The preacher was highlighting the significance of God's calling Abram away from his family and into a new land. The preacher included lots of details about Abram's hometown, Ur, as well as a brilliant overview of clan society and family expectations during Abram's day. But in the middle of that biblical history lesson, almost offhandedly, the preacher mentioned something else. He said the people of Ur were known to be astronomers.

Remarkable. *Astronomers!* And Abraham!

For half a minute or so, I looked around me excitedly to see if anybody else in the church had caught the significance of that detail. Astronomy! But it didn't seem they had. I waited some more. I expected it would be only a matter of time before the preacher enlightened them. But he didn't. I was shocked. Where in the world had this guy gotten his ministerial degree, anyway?

So I started silent-competitive preaching—that is, while in the process of listening to a sermon, I try to think of a better, more theologically sound and insightful sermon in my head. I like to think that I'm great at it.

My sermon on the Abraham passage was about reference points. It was about how God is so caring that at times he chooses to speak to people using words and experiences that seem specifically honed for those people's ears. It was about how he teaches us by making use of what's already significant to us but by flipping it or altering it somehow to make it newly and doubly significant. It was about a guy named Abraham who had grown up in a land where people loved stars, and it was about how God's promise to Abraham topped anything that even somebody from Ur could imagine: "Stars? *I'll* show you stars."

With that decided (and with my competitor's sermon having completed), I left the church feeling satisfied about what I had put together. My sermon not only had poetic potential, I thought; it also highlighted God's attentiveness and care for humans' small, everyday lives. Fantastic.

It wasn't until months later that I realized I didn't

deserve to win any preaching competitions; my astronomy analogy had zeroed in on a detail that was secondary at best. It was a good detail, a beneficial one, but it wasn't central. To get to the primary point, I needed to read one verse beyond the stars verse in Abraham's story. Or perhaps I needed to simply listen to the actual preacher's sermon, though there's no way to know for sure now.

The verse just after the stars verse says that through Abraham's offspring, all people everywhere will be blessed. This is the promise that carries down through centuries by way of the descendants of Abraham, Isaac, and Jacob. It carries on until it finds its completion in the one Descendant whose death and resurrection open up the door to ultimate blessing for all humanity. What the verse past the stars verse says is, in not so many words, Jesus.

Switch

THREE SPRINGS AGO

SOMETIME AROUND THE eight- or nine-week mark of the Honey Project, a phenomenon happened. Perhaps it's the type of thing that's common in fasting—I wouldn't know.

I was something like fifty or sixty days into the fast. The calendar read late March or early April, and barring a couple of mindless hiccups, I hadn't eaten anything artificially or processed-ly sweet, hadn't tasted so much as a pinch of everyday cane sugar in my tea, since the first of February. Instead I had been eating a lot of fruit. I had been drinking a lot of juice. I had been chewing mints in multiples and lacing my beverages with honey by the tablespoon.

It still felt painfully abnormal. I craved milkshakes. I craved birthday cakes. I craved things I hadn't craved since elementary school, like Ring Pops and candy necklaces. I craved things I wasn't sure I even liked, like tiramisu.

Then one day, out of nowhere and seemingly in an instant, everything was different. It was as if upon waking up that morning, the nature of my tastes and cravings had changed. When I made my way to the kitchen for a snack or a meal, rather than wanting cookie dough or fudge ice cream, what I wanted was tangerines, strawberries, honey, grapes. My hunger for sweets still seemed to strike just as often as always, but I no longer felt any desire to raid my cupboards on the chance of finding a lone jelly-bean or a stray chocolate chip. Suddenly my cravings were pointing me in new directions.

There was still more. Foods I had been eating since forever, never having given them a second thought, were out of the blue remarkably sweet. I could taste the sugar in carrots and ketchup, of all things, and in peanut butter and whole wheat bread. Even more amazing, when I would see a non-fruit dessert or treat—a plate of turtle brownies, for instance—I would feel a slight flip in my stomach, as if I might be getting sick. This was uncanny to me, and it seemed practically irreverent at first.

I wasn't sure what was happening, but my best guess seemed credible: when I started craving berries instead of chocolate, real juice instead of soda, and healthy sugars instead of snack-trash, it was because my taste buds were becoming un-tricked. My tastes were becoming more true. Before the Honey Project, when my body wanted sweet-ness, I gave it sugars in excess—and the wrong kinds of sugars. I had done this as long as I could remember: living on the cheap, sweet counterfeit version of what my body really wanted. Chocolate rather than berries, soda rather than juice, and so forth. I did this for plenty of reasons: the counterfeit was easier, it tasted good, I wanted to, PMS. Before the Honey Project, those habits seemed to work for me.

But unknowingly I had been training my body to want what it didn't need and shouldn't have. I was every day convincing myself to prefer the counterfeit over the real thing. This convincing seemed to happen all the way down to a cellular level, like a chemical dependence or an addiction. In the category of sweet things, I didn't know how to want the good stuff. My sense of taste was off, vastly. It had become a counterfeit itself.

This made me wonder: *What if my taste for God is off too?*

What if? It was a sobering question to consider. If the answer was no, it would mean a dead end in my search for God's sweetness, and I would have to search for some other route. If the answer was yes, it would be promising and maybe devastating. There would be hope that things could change between God and me—maybe I could learn to crave him after all!—but if my taste for God was off, it would mean that parts of my faith had been off balance for as long as I could remember.

Still, what if?

Not Testing the Lord

THREE SPRINGS AGO

IN EARLY SPRING of the Honey Project, I had to drop myself off at the airport. I was flying to the East Coast for a conference, and with both round-trip flights happening midweek, I hadn't been able to arrange for someone else to take me to the terminal and pick me up when I got home. I told myself that a woman with a boyfriend or a fiancé or a husband would've had her rides already built in.

Leaving a car in the long-term lot at Smallertown's nearest airport meant parking and then hauling my luggage through at least two parking lots before arriving at the check-in counter. Every time I had flown out of that airport in the past, the long-term lot had been packed— I had never once been able to find an open space in the

first section (the one closest to the terminal) and always
had to venture into far-away section two or, worse, section three. Then, since there was no shuttle system, I had
to pull a just-shy-of-fifty-pounds suitcase behind me, plus
my massive purse, a half mile in the early-morning dark.
Upon reaching check-in, I was always slightly sweaty and
haggard, breathless and with my back muscles aching. On
some of these occasions I had been concerned I might
appear to be a security risk.

Driving to the airport alone, knowing I would have to lug
my baggage and myself to the terminal alone, all the while
scanning the dark lot for creepy, lurking types who might
take advantage of a woman there alone, had always seemed
like an especially fitting time to mope about being single.
But on that day I didn't. Instead I thought about fasting, and
I decided to give God a wild opportunity to be sweet to me.
I asked him for my first-ever incredible airport parking space.

Two notes about that. First, I was the only person on
the planet who knew I was praying for a parking space, and
still I felt slightly embarrassed to do it. Second, there is a
verse in the Bible that says, "You must not test the LORD
your God."[1] It's a quote from Jesus, who is quoting a passage from Deuteronomy, so actually the verse appears in
the Bible more than once. It sounds foreboding, especially
when read in translations that use words like *thy* and *thou*
and *shalt*. If you are a person like me who enjoys obeying
rules, you read this verse and appropriately you think in the
imperative: *Do not, do not.*

I thought about the verse while exiting the highway for
Airport Road. I thought about how it shows up a plural
number of times biblically. I wondered what it meant to

test the Lord my God. I wasn't sure, so I follow-up prayed. With apology I explained to God that I wasn't sure I could emotionally handle lugging my luggage from the third long-term lot. I told him that I just wanted to believe honey could mean something. Then I took a time-stamped ticket from a machine at the entrance of the parking area, and I began pulling ahead. I felt trite and extremely bothersome.

But sure enough, on that day of all days, at least four, probably more, of the choicest spots in the first lot were open. I didn't even need to drive slowly to see them; the one I took was in the third row, directly across from the terminal entrance. I had never—I still have never—been able to park so close. It was magnificent and almost eerie, pulling onto that empty slab of asphalt.

As it turns out, I was going to have to get used to that kind of thing.

What happened next in my life was that men started climbing out of the woodwork. Some of them, astonishingly, even seemed interested in my company. During a dramatic week in late April, a man with whom I shared mutual friends emailed me to introduce himself. Days later, a second man (that time a man I had met) hinted he wanted the two of us to get together sometime. And then before the week was up, a third man (also one I knew) asked me on my first bona fide, non-blind date. The next weekend Guy #3 arrived at my house on time, not smelling of alcohol, without a felony record, and took me to dinner and a movie. A date. Suddenly I was occupying a new universe.

Then one week I talked with Cora about my debt; I did this only after having put together a long-term and foolproof payoff plan. I gave Cora the gruesome details, asked for her prayers as I tried to stick to my plan, and thought the conversation was done. In our talk the following Tuesday, Cora told me she had mentioned my debt to a friend of hers, and then she said that the friend had prayed about it and decided she wanted to cover the whole amount on my behalf, to help me find footing. Cora asked me whether that would be okay. I responded by crying and saying nothing for a long time; I had never been so humbled or moved. It took five or ten minutes before I could compose myself and think clearly enough to accept.

And I was asked for a third interview with a job in corporate communications; the position included zero writing about marital bliss and would allow me to say, "I work in marketing" rather than bringing up my first kiss upon being introduced to someone new. *Good-bye, unseemly self-disclosing small talk*, I thought. And only days after seeing an advertisement for the Perfect Apartment (outside Pumpkintown!), I had also met a potential roommate who could share the lease, so it seemed likely that both parts of a Perfect Living Arrangement would fall in place on a coordinating schedule.

This, *this*, was sweetness, I thought. It was proof that God is good. I hadn't done anything to deserve anything special—I had, in actuality, done plenty of things to *not* deserve anything special—yet there were special gifts in abundance. It seemed God was giving specific, delicate attention to me.

For a time I walked around in wonder of this, swept off my feet and bowled over by being wooed. My reaction was proof that I had some idea of what God was up to, and also that I had no clue.

Losing Franklin

THREE SPRINGS AGO

THREE WEEKS BEFORE my sister's wedding, on an early evening during the last week of May, I pulled into a Kentucky Fried Chicken drive-thru. I was thinking: *The order you're preparing to make is a grease pit.* And, *You already blew your budget for this month, and your apartment has plenty of food in the cupboards.* And, *You're going to walk into the funeral home smelling like a Fry Daddy.* But my week had had its fill of sorrows already. I didn't feel like adding hunger pangs to the list.

A mile away, Franklin lay stretched out in a casket. Making matters worse, in front of me was a Volkswagen Beetle with bumper stickers, three of them, and a little silver Jesus fish, to boot. If any one thing could've been

off pitch for the moment, it was that six-foot width of
a vehicle and its trio of slick sayings. I couldn't decide
whether looking at it was making me tired or just really,
really ticked off.

Four weeks earlier—less than thirty days—Franklin
had sat across the table from me in a Monday meeting
and mentioned that he'd put on weight. It was strange,
he'd said, but his voice had been even and he had smiled.
His doctor would do some tests. After a couple of days
somebody had called to say it was cancer, back with a
vengeance, and that had been the start of a quick ending.
Franklin's wife, Nettie, and all the kids and grandkids
had gotten together on a Saturday to take pictures. Three
weeks (a blink) later, he was gone. And so they were stuck
in a funeral home, missing him like their lungs had been
torn out, standing there waiting for people like me to
walk in and pay respects. Me, who respected him, who
felt something like love for him, but who couldn't possibly
remember the names of all six of his grandkids.

And yet. There I was, making the trip, about to interrupt their heartache with the offering of my own shallower
version. I wasn't sure how to feel about that—a little
sadder, maybe? A little guilty, a little relieved? Unsettled?
Mostly I just wished someone would muzzle that bumper
in front of me.

Sticker #1: green letters, white background, toward the
lower left side of the fender. "National Atheist Day," it said,
"April 1st."

The guy in the Volkswagen was looking at the big, plastic KFC menu and placing his order. I narrowed my eyes
to look through his rear window, noting first of all that

he was square-headed, with a haircut that was out of date. *Par for the course*, I told myself, looking away. I didn't want to make any more time in my week for people like him. *Religious and oblivious.*

The April thing had taken a minute to figure out, until I made the off-putting connection of April Fools' Day. After that, all I could do was picture the backward group of chums who had put their heads together to design the sticker. I confess, the personality profiles came together far too easily. Probably a conference table's worth of fifty-year-olds with stubby arms, I decided, and glasses that were a little too thick. At least one in the bunch believed PG movies were the antichrist, and the boss probably forgot to zip his fly all the time. How impossibly clever and hilarious they must've felt, a Bible-thumping brain trust who spent their time writing cheap, insulting slogans to blare out among exhaust fumes.

I shook my head and exhaled with a snort; the contradiction was maddening. *What possesses a person,* I wondered, *to not only purchase such a sticker but also claim the thing by affixing it to a vehicle?* While I'm no expert on bumper evangelism, it seemed obvious to me that there are more effective witnessing tactics than calling people fools. *Religious and oblivious.* As if I hadn't seen enough of that lately.

There had been a pastor in Franklin's hospital room when some friends and I visited the week before. The guy didn't have a clue what he was doing. Our group was there to say good-bye, to look Franklin in the face and thank him for all the ways his life had demonstrated God's brilliance. And we were there to hug Nettie, to stand beside her for a few minutes while she was losing her grandest love. As for Pastor What's-His-Name, I think he was there to be in charge of something and to prowl for sermon illustrations.

When we arrived, Franklin lay sleeping on the bed. His lips were chapped, and each breath he took was labored, noisy as it went in and out of his windpipe. A lone fluorescent bulb shone above his bed, making his hair seem bluish-gray against the whiteness of the pillow and emphasizing the loose, baggy skin on his neck and arms. It was startling to see my friend so thin—probably thirty or forty pounds gone, just like that.

"Time to wake him up?" asked a voice from the corner. Loudly.

I saw a man in his midforties seated in the corner chair. He was wearing crumply jeans and a rugby shirt too broad for his shoulders, and his face was eager, as if on the brink of a chuckle.

"What do you think, Nettie?" the man continued, still loudly. "Should we?"

I did not like him.

Furrowing my brow, I looked to Franklin's wife, doubtful that there could be an adequate explanation for Rugby's presence in the room. But Nettie didn't recoil or shoo him out like I wanted her to. She turned toward the corner where he sat, and she smiled. "I should introduce you to everybody."

Nettie called him by name, which was Roy or Dirk or maybe Ryan, and then she informed us of his occupation. "Fifth Church," the man cut in, grinning. "On the north side." After that he repeated his name several times, walking around and shaking all our hands wildly. An awkward silence followed, until Nettie spoke up briefly to say that the pastor lived in their neighborhood, a few streets away.

"Franklin and I met," the pastor offered, "one day when my kids were out selling candy bars for school." That grin of his—it was intolerable.

Franklin writhed on the bed, interrupting the conversation and my thoughts. He rolled his head from side to side; he struggled against the IV in his hand. Nettie took hold of his arm and began gently patting his shoulder in an attempt to wake him. But it was clear that the pain medication had made him confused and delirious; he didn't seem to know that other people were in the room with him, and he kept trying to take off his hospital gown, tugging at it like it was a giant necktie.

"Franklin," Nettie said. Loudly but softly, her face close to his. She pulled the thin cotton fabric back up toward his chin and held it there. "He gets so warm here," she explained with a smile. Her voice was calm. Her husband thrashed against the bed and tugged at his gown some more, but she kept it steady against his chest. "Your friends are here, Franklin. Do you see your friends?" He sighed, fluttered his eyelids in the direction of the ceiling, then followed her voice until his eyes found her face.

"Your friends are here." More quietly this time.

When Franklin had talked about his Nettie, he had always beamed with a certain level of amazement. Like a schoolboy with his first real crush, like a man who'd found a reason to be a hero. It had been adoration at its best, but now, after all their good years together, they were arriving at an ending. There in the hospital room he was frail and lost, a shadow of who he used to be, needing her to be tender and strong. I don't know how I witnessed the moment without falling apart completely.

"Does he like the food here?" the pastor wanted to know.

Dirk/Roy/Ryan had positioned himself at the center of the room, next to Franklin and opposite Nettie. It was impossible to ignore him. After asking his question, he gripped the bedrail and leaned over it possessively, looking first at Nettie, then back at the rest of us, then back toward Nettie again. With a meaningful nod, he signaled that she should direct her response to all the others, not to himself.

I remember admiring the way she maintained her poise then, and I remember that she answered the question with politeness, but I can't begin to recall what Nettie said. Her words, like so many other details from that afternoon, were drowned from my memory. Also forgotten: whether or not Franklin spoke at all during our visit or if he ever fully woke up. I wish I could remember. But from the moment the pastor took it upon himself to help update everyone on the patient's condition, my only clear recollections are of that man's ill-fitting shirt and his ill-fitting remarks and how he didn't deserve to be there and how angry I was.

He never seemed to stop talking, not even in all the time it took for Nettie to answer more of his ridiculous questions. And if he cared about what she was saying or how she felt, he didn't show it. He just stood next to my dying friend, making certain to interrupt every sentence with a knowing "Mm-hmm" or a ministerial "Mmnm" or some horrific combination of both.

"Does Franklin talk often? . . . Mmnm, mmnm."

"Have the doctors said anything new? . . . Mm-hmm."

"Is your church family being supportive? . . . Mm-hmm, mmnm."

"What's God teaching you right now? . . . Mmnm, praise the Lord."

It was all I could do to hold my tongue, and I had to concentrate every bit of my attention on the section of wall just above Nettie's outside shoulder. I found that by keeping my focus there I could limit the pastor to my peripheral vision and could almost convince myself that his actions and words were forgivable. Though I knew my reaction wasn't the kind of loving, dignifying one Franklin would've offered to someone carrying on like an imbecile, it seemed pretty good, considering that what I wanted to do was drop-kick the pastor out a window.

I tried to accept the fact that he wasn't going to exit, that we'd have to say our farewells with him running the show. In the middle of this effort, he cleared his throat. "You know what I think we should do," he said, still leaning over the bedrail, still grinning. "I think we should all go around the circle and share one reason why Franklin was special to us."

His words, when I'd digested them, hit me with a jolt. *Was*, he'd said. *Was*. Past tense.

"I'll start," he continued. Then he rolled back his shoulders, puffed out his chest, and in his best pastoral voice, he launched into his own one reason, without giving anybody else a chance to object to the idea. "Franklin always talked about his grandkids," was what he said. Past tense again. As if my friend were already gone, his sweet wife already a widow. As if the room, the hospital gown, the dying weren't happening right there in front of him.

The room fell silent. People looked at the floor, shuffled their feet, fidgeted with lint in their pockets. Nettie turned toward her husband and nervously untangled a tube connected to his IV needle. I clenched my jaw and balled my fists.

The pastor was beaming like a sultan; I knew it would be only a matter of time until people followed his lead. "*Is!*" I wanted to scream it at him. "Present tense—*is!*" So much grief, religion, and oblivion in one room. In the end, I said good-bye to Franklin without any idea how to.

Sticker #2, yellow and blue, in the middle of the bumper and directly beneath the Jesus fish: "Evolution Is Faith-Based."

While pulling up to the spot where I could order some chicken, I was aware of a voice in my head nagging me to ask for something other than just extra-crispy wings. "You can't eat only the skin," my mother had always told me with a frown, inspecting chunks of discarded chicken on my plate. "I don't want you to take another new piece until you've finished this meat."

The mature decision in ordering fried chicken, then as always, would've been to make sure the ratio favored the poultry rather than the oil-dunked fat. Not to mention other guilt trips: namely, my zero-balance food budget and the history of strokes in my family. Ultimately, though, the delayed-gratification arguments didn't hold up much against the fact that Franklin had died and I wanted some KFC. As a trade-off with my conscience, I included in my order a drumstick and a buttermilk biscuit, limiting myself to just a single crispy wing.

After easing around the corner of the building, I found

myself behind the Volkswagen bumper again. I slouched in
my seat and turned to look toward the brick wall outside
my window. I tried to avoid thinking about the stickers—
and about anything.

The visitation would be full of Christians—I didn't
want to go. "God works everything together for good,"
I was afraid they would tell me, nodding and tilting their
heads thoughtfully to one side. But my sadness was palpable, and to me it didn't seem that the loss would ever feel
anything but useless. I didn't want to hear chipper Bible
references, and I didn't want to hear people talk about all
the purpose they were seeing in Franklin's death. I figured
you can spiritualize your pain and create bumper stickers
denying it, and you can smile and say happy things and
buy tasty chicken dinners on credit, but in the end it will
turn out to be nothing more than smoke and mirrors. The
future will still be uncertain. Franklin will still be dead.
And the easy answers will be futile: all fat, no meat.

Sticker #3, white on black, far right. This one's a quota-
tion of C. S. Lewis: "You do not *have* a soul. You *are* a soul.
You *have* a body."

I was sick of being in line behind that vehicle. The
mixed messages—a Christian symbol alongside a cheap
shot, flawed rhetoric next to theological mastery—they
were too much. The quote was something I might have
found compelling on a normal day, yet in this drive-thru
context I couldn't bring myself to take it seriously. Even
genius suffers a nosedive when it's been stuck, slightly
askew, under a VW logo. I sighed and glared away again,
my index finger tapping out frustration on the automatic
window control.

The Beetle guy was getting his food order. One, two, three boxes made their way into his car, followed by a drink caddy. He loaded up the empty seat beside him, and as he did this I entertained the idea that he was not only ignorant but a glutton, too. While waiting for him to leave, I tried to figure out which Christian from my week was a bigger embarrassment to the rest of us: Pastor Rugby Roy or this guy. Having watched him drive off, I pulled forward with relief that he was finally, finally gone.

At the drive-thru window, the KFC kid didn't wait even a second for me to pay before handing over my order. That irritated me. I had to balance uncomfortably so as to take the box of food from him while also reaching up and holding out a twenty. But he stepped backward from the cash, sending me the kind of annoyed, bored look only a sixteen-year-old can pull off.

"That other car," he told me, nodding toward where the Volkswagen had been. "They said they wanted to pay for yours, too."

My arm and the money were suspended midair between my car and the building. The drive-thru kid looked at me and shrugged, then started assembling another order. It was nearly a mile to the parking lot of the funeral home, and the whole way there I was too stunned to know if I should laugh or sob.

Riding on Grace

THREE SPRINGS AGO

THE LESSON OF grace was taught to me in morsels; it came only a little bit and a little bit more at a time. Perhaps this was an arrangement that God worked out because he knew I would need some easing into it. Then again, maybe it always happens that way.

A week after the KFC incident my family was in San Diego for David's graduation into the Marine Corps. A few of us, myself included, were waiting at a bus stop on a side street. There weren't any vehicles in sight, and we had been waiting a few minutes, so as a joke my future sister-in-law Christi walked toward the curb and stuck out not just a thumb but a hip, too. She held her position for just a moment, but it was long enough for a big, white Cadillac to turn onto the street. The driver slowed the car and pulled up to the place where she stood. It seemed he had seen only her, not the rest of us.

Christi was nineteen, tall and slim and beautiful. I could see that the driver was in his forties or fifties; he had dark hair, an olive skin tone, and angular Middle Eastern features. My brother David was due, in all likelihood, to deploy to Iraq or Afghanistan in the next year. So my response to the driver's stopping next to the curb was, *What kind of middle-aged pervert. . . ?* followed closely by, *The people shooting and roadside-bombing Marines like my brother this very moment look like this man.* I wondered whether the driver had a sawed-off shotgun under the seat or a stash of date rape drugs in the glove compartment. I wondered whether he had personally helped fund Al-Qaeda.

But the driver lowered his passenger's side front window and spoke to my dad. The buses aren't running today, he said—it's a holiday weekend. He told us he had a limo license and could take all of us wherever we needed to go. The man was kind and convincing, and he gestured insistently, so after a while we got in and let him take us. He drove our whole family to the zoo, listening to our stories and telling some of his own. We discovered he was from Iraq, his name was Michael, and he owned a café near the bus stop where he had found us. At the entrance to the zoo, he wouldn't take any cash for the trip, and he offered to pick us up again when we were finished.

Later that night, after a cab ride back to our hotel, we searched out Michael's café and tried to order drinks as a thank-you. He wouldn't have it. He gave us drinks on the house and came out from behind the bar to sit with us. He kept the place open past closing, entertaining and fascinating us for three hours. He told us the movie *Pay It Forward* had changed his life. He said every day he tried to give away something to someone—apparently, even to a racist—to start a chain reaction of giving.

Okay, I told myself on the trip home from the West Coast. *Lesson learned.* After having been given to freely by those I had wronged so deeply—first Mr. VW Fried Chicken and now the driver of the Cadillac—I was sure I was finally getting it. The theological parallel seemed obvious: God's grace came to me not only in spite of the fact that I didn't deserve it but also at expense to himself, though I had wronged him with my sin. Now that I had seen what it looked like when such a costly gift was given unsparingly, I felt more grateful to God than ever. Surely this was true sweetness.

I felt changed, and I assumed the Honey Project had finished its work. All that was left to do was coast to the end. But what I had seen was just shallow shovelfuls; grace still hadn't dug down to the root. There were miles yet to unearth.

Chastity Belt

THREE SPRINGS AGO

THE SUMMER I was in sixth grade my church youth camp counselor told our cabin full of girls, "Make sure you don't ever lie down with a guy." She endorsed it as a surefire way for all of us to keep our roller coaster of hormones in check so we could stay virgins until we were married. At the time I thought of it as wise advice, pragmatic and extremely reasonable. On the morning after Sarah's wedding, I thought of it and felt an intense need for damage control.

For weeks leading up to Sarah's big day, I had repeatedly reminded God that the event had a lot of potential to turn out horribly for me. I had asked him to prevent that from happening; in particular, I had asked him to keep me from feeling jealous or ugly or lonely when the day came. I had asked God to help me celebrate Sarah and her love in order that the day might be a great one for her and maybe even good in my life too.

Tom and I were still together and prone on the couch when Bridesmaid Stephanie came in and found us there. Her expression registered surprise, seeing us like that, then amusement: "Well, don't you two look cozy!" she exclaimed. At this I propped myself up to lean over Tom's chest, replying, "Good morning!" with a wide smile, as if it were the most normal thing in the world. The words danced in the air after I spoke them, like a new normal or some sort of sham—I couldn't tell which.

Only minutes before Tom had taken my hand to toy with the ring I wear, my mom's mom's diamond cocktail ring. There were lots of charming things I could've told him about Grandma June and all the ways the ring reminds me of her. But when he said, "That's a pretty ring," his fingers turning it toward the light, I couldn't look him in the eye, and it rattled me just to come up with "Thank you."

I had lain awake all night on the couch next to Tom, waiting for it to happen—whatever it is that happens when you toss aside a commitment you thought was a cornerstone. It had been quiet in the house, sleep-dulled, but hours had passed and as far as I could tell, nothing had fallen to total shambles. Then from somewhere out beyond the lake house, daylight had snuck up over the trees and in through the windows, and it was time to clean and tidy the lake house, ushering the weekend to a close.

At first I walked a slow circuit between the kitchen and the living room, sorting the previous night's bottles into bags and tossing the guys' rented tuxes into a bundle. My thoughts were not nearly so simple to sort as plastic and glass versus aluminum. I went to the kitchen and leaned against the counter, and for a while I pushed around a pile of wedding hairpins. I moved them to the left, I moved them to the right, I divided them into clusters. I tried to picture how my life would have to change.

In the place behind my eyes, irreversible memories from the night before were playing like a slideshow. I had pulled away from Tom both times he kissed me. I had never thought to move my hands to his temples or rest them behind his neck like a seasoned kisser would. No, I had been frozen. I had been mute all night too. And I hadn't dared open my eyes, not once when he and I were lying so close. After the second kiss I had burrowed my face into his shoulder to ultimately stop things, but first—a nail for the coffin—I had kissed him back. I had kissed him as passionately as you can kiss a man while also remembering to keep your eyes scared shut and every other body part except your mouth immobile.

I arranged the hairpins in groups by color. There was a handful's worth or so for each of the bridesmaids there at the lake house: a blonde, a brunette, and a redhead, like the three of us were some kind of lame joke come to life. But I couldn't guess the punch line, and I couldn't find a way to get myself out of what I had gotten myself into.

The really bad thing was, the kissing back hadn't been a fluke or a moment of weakness, and it hadn't happened because of any sort of pressuring from Tom. Between kisses one and two, I had wanted to kiss him back. I had decided, despite being sure I would never marry this man, to kiss him back if I got another chance. The idea had made my spine tingle.

In the morning, however, even a mundane task like sorting hairpins agitated me. The house was filled with voices of bridesmaids and wedding guests and grooms-men—it seemed at once too loud and too quiet. *Get away, get away, get away,* I kept telling myself. But my car was still parked across town at the reception hall, and there was still cleaning that needed to be done.

The only choice was to keep working; however, group cleanup had already led to several casual run-ins with Tom the Groomsman Whom I Had Kissed.

While tidying up in the kitchen, I heard the sound of Tom's voice growing louder, coming closer to me. Instantly I turned away and let my feet carry me down a hallway in the opposite direction, which happened to be toward a bathroom. Ducking inside, I locked the door behind me. Then I stepped toward the sink and leaned against it, feeling the cool porcelain against my palms. Turning on the faucet, I watched the water splash and fall for a while. There was a mirror on the wall in front of me, but I was avoiding looking into it. I noticed instead the color of the tiles on the floor, the pattern of the rug around my toes, the tiny wrinkles down one side of my shirt. I saw the circling water and Grandma June's diamond ring. Then, kneading my hands together under the water, I let my gaze climb up from the sink until what I was looking at was my own self looking back at me.

I sized up my reflection for a full minute, maybe more, testing whether the two of us could be comfortable and safe with each other again. I was relieved to see, with all that had changed, that my appearance was still mostly familiar: same cleft in the chin, same tip of the nose, same freckle patterns. Yet there was something different in the expression—something fractured and fidgety.

The Lisa I had been up till then—the one who didn't get caught up, who didn't need damage control, who wouldn't wander into the gray area, who wouldn't lose herself with Tom the Groomsman, who certainly wouldn't press herself against him, breathless and startling, on a narrow couch in the middle of the night—it had been twelve hours and forever since I was that person. I had always thought God wanted me to be her, had assumed that if I stopped being her, there would be trouble and smiting. But when I looked at myself in the mirror that morning, I was shocked to find myself wondering whether *this* was more in line with his desires: I was finally meeting the real me.

Only Brotherly

THE CURRENT SPRING

SIMON PETER WAS the disciple of Jesus who, on the eve of Jesus' crucifixion, denied knowing Jesus three times. Jesus had told Peter in advance that the three denials would come from Peter's own mouth before a rooster crowed, but Peter had been adamant in his disbelief. "Even if everyone else deserts you," he had said, "I will never desert you."[1]

Later that same night Jesus was betrayed by Judas Iscariot, arrested, and interrogated by the Jewish high council. In that amount of time, in spite of himself, a certain Simon Peter gave three strong denials on three occasions when asked if he knew Jesus. The third time he got extra dramatic, calling down a curse upon himself if it were a lie. After that a rooster crowed, and Peter, remembering what Jesus had said, "went away, weeping bitterly."[2]

The Gospel of John records a later conversation between Jesus and Peter. The setting this time is fresh after Jesus' death and resurrection, on the shore of a sea, after Jesus and Simon Peter had had breakfast with some of Jesus' other disciples. This conversation involves another set of three— it's fascinating in English, and in Greek it's even better.

The English version:

> Jesus asked Simon Peter, "Simon son of John, do you love me more than these?"
>
> "Yes, Lord," Peter replied, "you know I love you."
>
> "Then feed my lambs," Jesus told him.
>
> Jesus repeated the question: "Simon son of John, do you love me?"
>
> "Yes, Lord," Peter said, "you know I love you."
>
> "Then take care of my sheep," Jesus said.
>
> A third time he asked him, "Simon son of John, do you love me?"
>
> Peter was hurt that Jesus asked the question a third time. He said, "Lord, you know everything. You know that I love you."
>
> Jesus said, "Then feed my sheep." [3]

Why did Jesus keep asking the same question? Why was Peter hurt on the third ask? And what do sheep have to do with it? In trying to make sense of all this, I've found that a Greek concordance comes in handy.

It's important to note first of all that the Gospel of John was originally written in Greek. It's also important to note that biblical Greek encompasses not just one but three words for the English word *love*. There is *eros*, which is sexual love; *phileo*, or brotherly love; and *agape*, which is self-giving, action-oriented love. In the post-breakfast encounter between Peter and Jesus, more than one type of love appears.

The Greekified version:

> Jesus asked Simon Peter, "Simon . . . , do you *agape* me . . . ?"
> . . . Peter replied, "You know I *phileo* you."
> "Then feed my lambs." . . .
> Jesus repeated . . . : "Do you *agape* me?"
> . . . Peter said, "You know I *phileo* you."
> "Then take care of my sheep." . . .

Some biblical commentators suggest that in this chapter the three questions of Jesus offer a gracious second at bat for Peter, a chance for him to redeem himself after his three denials. But it's not certain that the conversation is quite so tame, because it's possible to read a bit of bite in Jesus' questions. In his third question of Peter, the one that leaves Peter hurt afterward, Jesus switches up his Greek:

> "Simon . . . , do you *phileo* me?"
> . . . "You know that I *phileo* you."

It is an interaction that could be viewed as another loss for Peter the denier: Christ gives him the chance to offer all he has back to God, and Peter stops short at brotherly love and won't man up to full *agape*. But perhaps such a view is not reading the passage through the lens of full grace.

Here we have a man who only days earlier had with

confidence and maybe cockiness put stock in his own ability to follow Jesus boldly. "Even if everyone else deserts you, I will never."[4] There were, perhaps, valid reasons for Peter to believe he could pull that off—he had already given up his career and left his family to follow Christ around the countryside for who knows how long—probably years. He had once gone out on a limb and had, in front of all the other disciples, dared to say that Jesus was the Son of God. On top of that, he had attempted to walk on water and for a short time had even managed it. His discipleship to that point had demonstrated gall and a fierce tenacity, no doubt. Even so, in a few gray moments before dawn, he found he was still fundamentally lacking and wrong. At an hour of hours, when his beloved rabbi was being fed to wolves, Peter couldn't keep even one denial down his throat.

It's all so relatable.

Jesus says of himself, "I am the good shepherd. The good shepherd sacrifices his life for the sheep."[5] What he means is *agape*, demonstrated with sharp nails through hands and feet. *Agape*, hanging there until the last breath is gone. *Agape*, the only way for sinful people to stand before a holy God. *Agape*, the only purely good love, the only good.

But I tend to look at myself and think, *Good too*. Good at following God more than most other folks. Good at holding my tongue for the most part. Good at being an example, especially when there's a stage to stand on. Good at celibacy and virginity. Good at not needing forgiveness most days. Good at making up for my flaws and foibles. Extra good at not kissing anybody. It is a story cut from the same stone as Peter's "I will never," and somewhere there is a rooster about to crow.

The prediction Jesus made about Simon Peter is one that can be echoed universally to each one of us: *You will deny me.* It is a reality we cannot escape, even in our best goodness. We will deny Christ at the most important times and in the most important places. We will deny him with our behavior and with our words. We will deny him even as we consider the thought *I will never.* We will kiss the near stranger on a narrow couch with a rum and Coke in our system, and afterward we will look for ways to make it fixable. We will do this because we don't understand our sin—that it goes beyond just an unfortunate pattern in our lives, down to our very nature and fundamental reality. We'll relegate grace to a footnote, barely needed in the story.

But no. This mind-set is a poor counterfeit of the rich thing, holiness. It suggests in subtle and blatant ways that a life in Christ is something to be accomplished, like making the honor roll or swallowing the biggest pie at a picnic. It says faith is something to be good at, a reason to excel. But the marrow of faith is not human achievement or moral behavior. It is not a status to be earned, and it is not a résumé to be built. At the root of a life transformed by Christ, there is only this: my needing him absolutely, and knowing that I do.

Part of the message of Christ's death, God's sacrificing his own Son for humanity, is that even at our best and brightest, at our most spot-on and well-intentioned, we are incapable of being the people we would need to be in order to get to God. So I am more than just a person who sins; I am a sinful person. On my own I am fundamentally, unchangeably full of sin, no matter how good I try to get. My only hope for a future apart from my sin is to accept the one gift I can never deserve: Christ's sacrifice.

It is an ugly sort of arrangement if you're looking for balance. It is a painful thing to accept when you've been working to make your way on your own. Perhaps this is why Jesus' *agape/phileo* exchange with Peter has hurt in it: for someone who is trying to hang her hat on *good*, grace feels almost humiliating at first.

Agape? Jesus wanted to know, and Peter said, essentially, "I can only *phileo*."

Agape? Jesus had asked again, and Peter had said again, "Sorry, just *phileo*."

Okay, *phileo then*, Jesus wanted to know, almost more a statement than a question. "Yeah, *phileo*," Peter said.

The story may be more than this too, but it is certainly not less: Peter had learned he could no longer expect to perform flawlessly. He had seen *agape* in action, and he had also seen the total failure in himself. Peter understood his capacity and his limitations; he knew when he couldn't offer more. He could never love like his rabbi did.

"God's admiration for us," Saint Francis of Assisi writes, "is infinitely greater than anything we could conjure up for him." But here is the amazing thing. After *agape* and *phileo* go back and forth around a fading breakfast camp-fire, Jesus responds to Peter a third time: "Feed my sheep." Why feeding sheep? Because the Good Shepherd is good, and he is looking for apprentices. If that's not clear enough on its own, two verses later Jesus tells Peter, "Follow me."[6] This is a repeat of how Jesus first invited disciples into discipleship with him, so maybe it signals something of a fresh start. Then again, maybe it's just a continuation of the same story.

"I can manage *phileo*," the disciple says. "My *agape* doesn't come close."

Jesus doesn't argue the point; it seems he will take *phileo*. He says, "Follow me. I still want you to be mine."

Signed Up

THREE SPRINGS AGO

SINCE THE DAY my little brother David announced he had
signed up as a Marine Corps recruit, I had wanted to talk
him out of it. This wasn't because I minded Marines or
took issue with war entirely. No, I could appreciate that a
position in the military could make someone healthier and
stronger and more disciplined—all good things. People
would yell at David in boot camp, I figured, but younger
brothers can usually handle that. As to the moral and
philosophical side of things, while I wanted to believe peace
among fallen humans could be always achievable without
some kind of army, I had never been able to take that argu-
ment to its logical end without having it fragment royally.
This case has been made ad nauseam: Hitler. Let's imagine,
as the phrase goes, killing him with kindness.

When David enlisted, the war in Iraq had been going on for several years but had been at its bloodiest the previous year. One news article I remember seeing around that time was about an hours-long shoot-out that left several Marines blown to pieces by heavy gunfire and grenade blasts. I read only the article's headline and a couple of photo captions, and I needed to stop there. I worried if I went any further I would vomit.

My theory about war as an unfortunate necessity wasn't working in the same way now that my little brother was thrown into the mix. On top of that, it seemed obvious enough that David's decision, while honorable, was for him also entirely ignorant. He must've been charmed by those "the few, the proud" commercials, by the snappy traveling drill team and the dress blues, by the recruiting sergeants who ran lunchtime pull-up competitions in his high school cafeteria. He couldn't possibly have thought it through.

It baffled me that someone could be flippant with so weighty a decision. This wouldn't be summer camp, and there were far less potentially costly ways to prove one's manhood. How could he not see that he would be going to war? Tanks, suicide bombers, IEDs, missiles, and M16s would become his daily realities. He would have enemies, and he might be somebody's living target. None of it was a right fit for anybody, especially not David. He was a good-natured, easygoing kid. I still called him Davey sometimes, and he still let me get away with it. His cheeks were still rosy and a little chubby.

I had mentioned my concerns to David once, in a serious, sisterly speech about the realities of gas chambers and Kevlar. He responded simply and patiently, saying he liked the idea of doing something for honor, that he knew the Marine Corps was where he wanted to be. So I kept my worries to myself. I bought a USMC T-shirt online, got excited with him about military abbreviations, and agreed with him often that the Marine Corps commercials were the best ones out there. It still didn't make sense to me, but I was keeping my mouth shut.

Then one day shortly before he went to boot camp, David surprised me by showing up at my office and bringing me lunch. He strode in, gave me a hug, then claimed a seat across from me at my ghostwriter desk while we ate. He was funny and I laughed. It was a typical interaction between the two of us. But then, about fifteen minutes into our lunch, I realized that outside my door, the office seemed to be bustling more than usual.

My first assumption was based on the fact that David was six feet five and under thirty—I figured some of the office ladies had noticed a tall young man was talking to me, and they were hanging around to swarm for details and gossip when I walked him out. I decided to keep them waiting out of spite. But when we were finished with lunch and it was time for David to go, I opened my office door and instantly saw it was the office men, not the women, who were standing in our way. Apparently word had gotten around that Lisa's visitor was David, the Marine recruit.

"Hey, it's David," said Mark, the one guy in the office who had met him before. Mark said this oh-so-nonchalantly, as if he hadn't been hovering in the vicinity for that express purpose. The others took this as their cue and dropped whatever busywork they had taken up outside my door. "Thanks for what you're doing," they kept telling him. "Thank you." David shook their hands. His shoulders were back, his posture strong, his expression confident as he looked them in the eyes. There was nothing flippant or ignorant about it. It was only grave. The graveness was what stunned me.

Things shifted for me in that instant. Suddenly I realized that all the savagery of war—brokenness and separation and atrocity and death and the doing of unspeakable things—was about to be carried on my baby brother's back. On a pair of arms that hadn't yet been able to manage more than three pull-ups at a time. Looking at David then, for the first time since his enlistment, I considered a new possibility. When it came to the question of danger and pain and the finality of life, perhaps my brother didn't see less than I did. Perhaps he was the one who saw more.

Days later, when David was about to leave town, I drove over to my parents' house for a good-bye. I tried not to think about the men in the office. I tried not to think about bullets and explosives and blood. Instead I stood on tiptoe to hug my brother's neck tightly, and I held on much longer than usual. I told him I loved him and that I was so, so proud. I cried and cried because he was my kid brother, and because I was afraid and worried and sad. When he was gone I drove home with puffy eyes, feeling perhaps more in awe of him than I had ever felt of anyone.

My brother's service in the Marines wouldn't be limited to sacrifice alone; he would have regular compensations and perks: a reliable paycheck, the GI bill for schooling, free travel, an automatic gym membership, and military discounts. Which is to point out the obvious fact that David's sacrifices, both the real ones and the potential ones, are just a glimmer of ultimate self-sacrifice. Just a hint of the real thing. Still, Christ's sacrifice is so powerful that even hints and glimmers of it will knock people off their feet. This is why, when somebody signs up to stand in harm's way, others fall all over themselves to express gratitude. They line up and they shuffle their feet with undeservingness while shaking the kid's hand. Things feel out of balance, but at the same time things feel somehow right, because in the light of such sacrifice, all else becomes "Thank you."

Sexy, Cursing, Drinking Phase

THREE SPRINGS AGO

AFTER MY FIRST two kisses and after I experienced God's grace in the aftermath of them, I felt absolutely liberated. The freedom of not having to earn my own standing with God was richness to me, and I wanted to spend it. So I went out and bought not only my first-ever bikini but also a bottle of fingernail polish that was fire-engine red, and I found occasion to wear both almost immediately. At a party I drank two and a half rather strong mojitos without getting paranoid about whether or not I might get slightly tipsy. (As it turned out, I did.) I used an off-color, foul-ish word (previously banned from my vocabulary) in conversation. I said it once, twice, three times—without even flinching. I became for a while the sort of example that wise mothers are wary of.

The phase didn't last long; whiplash never does. Over time I discovered that reveling in God's grace didn't necessarily require emphasizing how crude and irresponsible I could be. When the dust settled, I had returned to careful behavior, to pursuing obedience as best as I could. Things looked mostly the same as before, despite the fact that everything was brand new.

My sexy, cursing, drinking phase may have looked like rebellion or misbehaving, like a faithful Christian turning lenient and losing her way. It wasn't. I had no interest in playing fast and loose with grace, and I didn't want a religion that was permissive and weak. Still, when I went back to my familiar actions and obedience, this time something had fundamentally shifted in my perspective.

Here is what I mean: In the months of the Honey Project that were pre-couch, pre-kissing, there had been a handful of occasions when I had broken my fast by mistake. During month three, for instance, I met a friend at a coffee shop and habitually ordered my favorite drink on the menu: a hot chocolate with extra whipped cream. I sipped half the mug before it crossed my mind that both hot chocolate and whipped cream are undeniably sweets. Guilty, I left the rest of the mug unfinished. I avoided mentioning my fast for the rest of the meeting.

A few weeks later I ran into some friends I hadn't seen in years. They offered to take me out to their favorite little bistro so we could all catch up. On a whim I agreed, only to walk in the door of the place and find it served only dessert. This flummoxed me. I didn't want to offend my friends by not placing an order; at the same time, I didn't think I knew them well enough to get into the intimate details of why I was fasting. So I ordered the least sweet dessert on the menu—a fruit-based caramel torte—and as with my first failure, I made sure not to finish it.

A couple of months after that, on the day of Sarah's wedding and on the night of her all-dessert reception, I neglected to bring a supply of fast-friendly food with me. On top of that, during the time set aside for pre-wedding dinner, I got caught up in ceremony details and skipped the buffet. As a result, by the time I was about to be called on to give a toast at the reception, I was more than a little lightheaded. To ward off possible fainting, I ate the strawberry parts of two chocolate-covered strawberries, and I had a few bites of plain cheesecake. I spread a napkin over my plate after that, to help myself keep from eating what was left.

After The Kiss, I finally accepted that no act of goodness—refusing the last half of a torte, for instance—could make my sinfulness less offensive, less entire. I was accepting the gospel message that says God can love me fully, even when I'm in the throes of violating my word to him. I was admitting to myself that my level of deservingness would never climb above an even zero.

"If the mercy is true," wrote Martin Luther, "you must therefore bear the true, not an imaginary sin. God does not save those who are only imaginary sinners. Be a sinner, and let your sins be strong."[1] For a time I took my extra-good works completely off the table, and I let my faith stand only on the merit of God's love and sacrifice. This allowed me to define myself not as someone impressively faithful but as someone rescued. It was humbling, and it was heaven.

This is the scandal of grace: the jolt that comes afterward is not from the heaviness of remorse but from a new, tender lightness. I was learning how to be less and infinitely lower than I had always expected and thought I was. I was beginning to see what it means to be drawn to God—not committed out of mere duty, not faithful simply because it might cajole him into favor, but attracted to him and won over by the reckless extent of his love.

Part Five

By Flock

Strong Again Faster

THE CURRENT SPRING

THERE IS A black-and-white photograph of my grandma, my dad's mom, as a young woman with her hands on her hips, and it should be noted that one of those hips is cocked sassily to the side. Gram is standing alone in a grassy field, wearing short sleeves and cotton overalls, with a straw hat framing her spunky, fearless face. The photo is dated 1938. Its caption says, "Anne after hoeing pickles all day." In the picture, Gram's expression says nothing of how hot workdays can put a burn in the back of your neck, crimps all down your spine, and a scream in your forearms. The look on Gram's face is triumphant and defiant: it says she could lick another crop's worth, with pleasure.

Gram is eighty-eight now. She has been white haired

and widowed for over two decades, and she seems shorter today than she used to be. Still, up till a little over a year ago, it seemed she hadn't changed much since the pickle field. She had her sturdy work ethic and her stout demeanor, and she could run circles around most sixty-year-olds. Gram volunteered on Tuesdays, played chauffeur when her aging girlfriends needed a ride to the salon, and hooked worms to go fishing with her great-grandkids whenever she got the chance. She played cards with her neighbors and offered sharp critiques of her young preacher's sermons if his theology seemed skewed. She put her wrinkled, eight-and-a-half-decades-old body into a bathing suit once a week for water aerobics down at the local university pool. Sometimes Gram cussed just to be funny. She was endlessly spry, same as ever.

But then one day she had a small, rude stroke that left one of her legs partially paralyzed and threw off her balance once and for all. At the ER in the days that followed, Gram's doctors mandated that some precautions be made for her everyday safety. In case of another stroke and to avoid falls, they said Gram needed to either (1) stop living alone or (2) outfit her place with a collection of occupational health gadgets. Between the two there was no contest.

Determined to keep both her condo and her independence, Gram made sure every item on her prescribed list was meticulously accounted for: Grip bars screwed into her bathroom walls. Nonslip rugs laid on all her linoleum floors. A handrail installed next to the stoop in her garage. A lockable gate attached to her banister to prevent stairway falls. When Gram's doctors insisted that she start using a walker or a cane at all times, even at home, Gram ordered a cane in floral pastels and the snazziest, most high-tech walker she could find—she calls it her Cadillac—in pink. Then, the hospital discharge papers approved, she went home and made a point of teetering around her condo without holding on to anything.

Obstinacy wasn't her focus, at least not fully so. What Gram wanted was to be independent and to stay that way—she was insistently not in favor of moving to an assisted living center. So on top of repeatedly snubbing both cane and Cadillac, nearly every day she did twice the number of physical therapy exercises her doctor had recommended. She hoped this regimen would make her strong again faster. Sitting in her La-Z-Boy, she would lift her heels off the floor, then her toes, then her heels again, then her toes again. She wasn't sure, but occasionally she thought that maybe she had felt something in her leg afterward, in the paralyzed part.

Gram's doctors had given a prognosis that wasn't promising; still, everybody else was at least partly willing to take her word over something scrawled on a medical chart. Gram had always been capable and determined, always with plenty of pluck for the task at hand. So even the most pessimistic among us believed Gram could push through and soon enough end up laughing on the other side.

That was over a year ago. It was at the start of a long, hulking winter. Snow came and didn't stop coming; it piled up and drifted and made the roads treacherous for weeks on end. After that, for months every horizontal surface— tree branches, driveways, lawns, lakes, any roof of anything—was covered in thick, heavy white.

Under the eaves of one particular snow-weighted condo, Gram's strength and energy were fading rapidly away. The woman who had tirelessly hoed her pickle rows was now getting winded going up or down stairs. She could no longer push the vacuum. She had even lost her energy for cooking. Even more disturbing, Gram was forgetting to take her blood pressure medication sometimes. On a few occasions she had accidentally doubled up on a day's supply. Her walking was also becoming slower and more difficult than ever—several times already, stepping one unsteady foot after the other toward the bathroom, she wasn't able to get herself there quickly enough. On the days other people were in the house with her when this happened, the cleanup process was humiliating for Gram. On the days when no one else was around, who knows how much time and tiredness it took for her to scrub her soiled clothes and floors alone.

"Gettin' old ain't for sissies," she started to say. At first she had said it with a chuckle each time, making light of things. But then as her physical strength and her emotional toughness began to wear thin, other pieces lost some of their luster too. Now the hardest part of this isn't Gram's forgetfulness, tiredness, repeated sickness, or unsteadiness on her feet. It's the simple fact that her chuckle has stopped materializing. "Gettin' old ain't for sissies," she says, and then she gives only a smile and a long, tired sigh.

Gram has been sighing a lot lately. A few weeks ago, after a particularly bad infection left her gaunt and weak and especially sad, her kids decided to go against Gram's wishes and move her out of her condo for a while. My parents picked Gram up on a Sunday afternoon, packed a suitcase for her, and brought her home with them. They gave her their main floor bedroom so she won't have to manage the stairs, installed a grip bar and a shower chair in their bathroom, and put down nonslip rugs in their kitchen. The plan is that she'll stay for a month or two at least, until the weather is warm again.

One might think that Gram would be only pleased and relieved about this arrangement, now that there are others in the house every day, helping to remember medication schedules and taking away the burden of meal prep, bringing her mugs of hot tea and glasses of water to keep infections down, gently holding her elbow on walks from the living room to her bedroom. My dad is having a hoot watching *Wheel of Fortune* with her every night, for instance. And my mom has been building a homespun spa routine for Gram's feet—whenever I visit, there are delighted reports that the cracked heels are beginning to soften again.

In time, other improvements become noticeable as well. Gram goes a couple of weeks without an out-of-control infection. Her legs are beginning to feel better because every day her pressure socks are pulled all the way up to knee-high, a chore Gram can't manage on her own anymore. She's eating three good meals a day again: the hollows of her cheeks are rounding out, and she laughs because her butt is rounding out too. Gram appreciates all this. The constant company and regular care allow her to feel relaxed in many ways, and she says so. But in some aspects it's only making things heavier for her; you can see that in the stooping of her shoulders and the shaky hesitance of her gait.

Gram talks a lot about being a burden. She worries about it. In at least half of her conversations, at some point she mentions how much she can't wait to do things for herself again, to stop taking such a toll on everyone. Invariably whoever is talking with her says that it's no burden, that her whole life Gram has been a great mom and grandma and sister and friend, that it's a joy to give her these small gestures in return. Without exception Gram shakes her head and furrows her brow. She looks down at her hands. She sighs one of her long, tired sighs.

At first Gram's response to help is something I think I don't understand. I tell myself it's unreasonable to turn down something you need, something good and beneficial, when another is offering it. I tell myself all this using fluffy, pious terms and recalling the wonder of grace. What I don't think about is the reality of accepting that grace, how awful it feels, or how difficult it must be for Gram. Neither do I spend time considering how thick this blood is that's shared between us.

Busy Household Bandit

THE CURRENT SPRING

SEVERAL MONTHS INTO community living, and several
more months into work on my manuscript, even the most
optimistic progress report is barely worth mentioning. The
book draft is still nowhere near complete, and the deadline
is nearer than ever. The only headway I seem to be making
is that I've begun to own up to some of the time-thieving
reasons why.

At the farm I am trying hard to chip in and be part
of things. The KMJs keep insisting that I shouldn't feel
obligated, and I keep insisting that I don't. But the truth
is, during hours when I should be writing, sometimes I'm
looking for chores to do or finding ways to prove myself
useful. Sometimes I am being farm-social to a degree I can't

afford. And every night after dinner (which I sometimes chip in to help cook), I plant myself at the kitchen sink and scrub all the pots and pans until they're gleaming. I take too much time out on weekends to play with the kids, and I have extended conversations with Kay in the kitchen. I make elaborate meals and snacks, and first I take long trips to the grocery store to find the necessary ingredients. Once I spent two hours of a stormy Saturday helping move The Ladies and their paddock from one muddy field to another.

I'm doing these things because I like to, because sometimes a girl just wants to be domestic or outdoorsy. But mostly I'm doing them because I don't want to become an offense or a burden. I'm doing them because I don't want to be seen as the household food bandit. I'm doing them because I am forever and irrationally afraid of being sidelined and unwanted.

At the office there's a similar fix. My team is overloaded with exciting possible projects, and I find myself wanting to attempt and brilliantly execute all of them. The stack of ongoing work at my desk is always bigger and more demanding than I can handle. I am taking meetings on the fly, and I'm rushing, sometimes running, from one assignment to the next. Thus I have labeled my intake folders based on when I'll realistically have time for them: "Later" and "Much Later." I'm getting in before hours, staying after hours, and not taking a lunch break. When I arrive home at the end of a day, there's about enough creativity left to fill a teacup.

I'm in need of a different solution, in need of finding more hours for working on the manuscript. There's a signed agreement, after all, and "breach of contract" has

an ominous ring to it. So apparently I'm getting desperate.
I've considered quitting my job, being a starving artist who
lives off rice and noodles and a skimpy savings account
for a few months. This is a horrible idea: the employment
market is awful, I don't have enough financial cushion to
make it anyway, and I'd feel disgusting if I ate so many
refined carbs.

I've also debated trying to land an easy, uncreative job
that's closer to home and won't leave me sapped and spent.
This possibility is not promising either. I love my work,
and with a looming deadline it would be nonsense to take
time writing résumés. Besides, living on the farm means
every other location would be a commute. I've also thought
about moving away from the farm, moving back in with
my parents. They're fantastic, but at this stage in my life,
I don't think I could swallow my pride enough to go back
to my old pink bedroom.

So here I am, searching fruitlessly for a solution, and
I am stumped by an old dilemma: more people only com-
plicate things further. Don't they?

Hide-a-Fast

AT THE START of the Honey Project, one of my goals had
been to not make many announcements that I was fasting.
I would keep quiet about the fast almost entirely, I had
thought. I would go to my ghostwriter office during the
day and out with friends or family at night, and whenever
I had to turn down sweets, I would do it as discreetly as
possible. Six months later, just as quietly, I would stop fasting, and most people would be none the wiser. In making
this plan, however, I neglected to consider a few things.

One: Food brings people together.

Two: When people get together, they bring food.

Three: Where I come from, they usually bring sweets.

It's nearly impossible to hide a fast—I am now willing

to submit that this is true universally. Eating, it seems, is by nature more of a group event than an individual activity. Even in my mostly boring single life, this was evident right away. It caused problems right away too.

What I learned: Something as simple as bringing a brownie-free lunch to work or passing on a slice of cheese-cake at a party is something people are inclined to notice and care about. They will possibly view this as a social affront, a combative one. In these cases, they will poten-tially respond by talking about their body weight and/or exercise regimen, all while turning red faced and defensive.

During the first week of the fast at a buffet dinner, several of my acquaintances asked if I was on a diet. I responded, confused, "No, I'm not." When they pressed further, pointing out all the pastries and cookies that were absent from my plate, I admitted that I wasn't eating sweets. With that, suddenly the discussion turned to love handles, spare tires, and extra inches. People kept saying, "I *really* need to lose some weight."

This pattern continued, no matter how much I tried to minimize the Honey Project or keep it a secret. I was mystified. My fast seemed to have a voice of its own, and somehow it always seemed to be calling people fat. But the most frustrating aspect of this unintentionally public fast was precisely that: the public part.

Of the reasons I had wanted to keep the fast to myself, there is one that is noble: my giving up sweets for a while was something between God and me. It wasn't intended to be some kind of a show. But there were other reasons why I wanted privacy. I wanted it because I was worried about my chances of succeeding.

The fewer people who knew I was fasting, the fewer people would have to know later if I botched the plan and ended up gorging on triple-layer cake or fudge sundaes. In the same way, if I didn't divulge to others that I was fasting, then in conversation there would be no easy, casual transition into the details of my floundering spiritual life. "Hi, I'm Lisa. I'm not eating these here sweets because I can't stop being mad at God." This was not a topic I was eager to bring up in conversation.

In Judgment

THREE SUMMERS AGO

A FEW MONTHS before the Honey Project began, long before I joined the staff and still in my early days of being part of the Mars Hill community, there had been a definitive moment when I almost bailed on my church.

It was a summer Sunday, I remember, and two of our pastors were tag-team preaching. Halfway during their sermon, in an offhanded and mostly unrelated comment, one of them mentioned his favorite beer by name. It was not an alcohol-free beer. People listening from the chairs laughed like crazy at this. I was so horrified I nearly choked on my own spit.

By that time I had belonged to not one but three church communities where one of the membership requirements was to be alcohol free. At the evangelical university I had attended, all students signed an agreement saying they wouldn't touch a drop. Now here was a *pastor*! In *church*! With a *microphone*! Saying that he *drank*?! Didn't these people know that verse about not becoming a stumbling block?

It was almost too much for me. For a few seconds my heart rate registered spiking levels of angst, and no doubt a look of judgment and hoity-toity suspicion flashed across my face. I instantly questioned whether anybody in this church had even a partial grip on holiness. After the service I nearly left for good. Nearly, but not quite.

At the time I couldn't have given clear, sensible reasons for staying, but I knew I couldn't bring myself to leave, either. This lasted for several months. On many occasions I asked myself whether being a part of Mars Hill meant I had gone religiously berserk. I worried that under its influence I might become far too lax and lenient to be spiritually respectable. But I stayed.

Then came a day that was half a week after Sarah's wedding and the kissing and everything. It was a Tuesday, and I was due to call Cora. I picked up my phone to start dialing, but for a few minutes my fingers were stubborn about punching in her number.

Together Cora and I had been praying about the wedding for months; now that the day was over, I knew she would ask me about it. Cora, who had championed the direction of my life up till that point. Who had asked me to mentor her two nieces about relationships, for goodness' sake. Who had given both girls signed copies of *Saving My First Kiss*.

All things considered, I wondered how many pages of the nieces' books would need to be ripped out and burned. I wondered how horrified and justifiably hoity-toity my friend would be.

After finding the nerve to actually call, I managed to make chitchat about the wedding for five minutes while trying to get brave. Then Cora asked a few chitchat follow-up questions, which bought me a little more time. My answers were drawn out, lengthy. I was stalling.

I felt a sense of responsibility to Cora. What if she felt let down? What if she felt led astray? What if she decided her beloved nieces had been duped by a phony? I hated the idea of being such a disappointment, and I was bracing myself for the worst-case scenario: a string of long-lasting, multi-pronged apologies.

Getting around to the facts of the wedding took me about twenty-five minutes. First there had been a lot of stuttering and directionless preamble.

"Actually, something happened . . ."

"I didn't expect it, but . . ."

"It was at this house . . ."

"I don't like telling you this . . ."

"Looking back, I should've caught on . . ."

"I hate disappointing you or anyone else . . ."

"Well, I was just so naive . . ."

I was worked up and jittery and practically lightheaded. Or perhaps I was just feeling really, really guilty. And since grace was still such a new work in my life, I didn't know how to expect that someone could respond to me graciously.

To Ashes

THE CURRENT SUMMER

ASH WEDNESDAY, though a noted date on the traditional Church calendar, is not formally observed by many evangelical churches. In my West Michigan neck of the woods, for instance, most Christians think this day is for Catholic types only. Most of us grew up without knowing what Ash Wednesday is about. We've never practiced it, and we have no problem finding it odd and a little creepy.

Before Mars Hill became part of my life, my only formal experiences with the Church calendar had been the more or less standard observances: Advent, Christmas, Lent, Palm Sunday, Good Friday, Easter. Sometimes not even Advent and Lent. None of the churches I had been part of in the past had been big on liturgy—when it came to practicing sacred rites and rituals, we were willing to light purple and pink candles around Christmastime each year, but that was typically as wild as we got.

There is a practice on Ash Wednesday called the giving and receiving of the ashes. Traditionally the ashes are burned fronds from the previous year's Palm Sunday—those who come to receive the ashes expect to have that fine, gritty palm dust put on their foreheads. They wear it all day in the shape of a cross, given in two small smudges by someone else's ash-covered thumb. This is a way of remembering and mourning. We remember Christ's time of temptation in the wilderness and we mourn his death. And we remember and mourn our own dying: the fact that death and sinfulness rule us finally, that even at our best we are full of the deceit and ingratitude and arrogance and self-motives that put holiness on our own strength permanently out of reach. It is a fine, gritty reality.

My first Ash Wednesday service, technically speaking, happened just a few weeks into the Honey Project. Leading up to the service, I kept hearing announcements about it, and with each one I became more relieved that I already had plans to be out of town that day. Truth be told, I questioned whether the service was necessary. It seemed like overspiritualized fanfare—silliness, even. And all things being equal, I wasn't thrilled about looking like I had dirt on my face.

The next year, the Ash Wednesday just after the Honey Project and just before I joined the staff, we had a service too. That time I didn't have a prescheduled excuse not to be there. Plus, I was a volunteer leader with a small group of high school students at the time, and those girls asked me to go with them. Feeling I had little choice in the matter, I went.

There were several hundred people there, maybe a thousand. We sang, prayed, and read Scripture together for a little while, then a group of people holding small bowls of ashes walked to the edge of the stage. The rest of us formed lines moving toward them, and person by person we were smudged. "From ashes you came," the givers said—vertical smudge—"to ashes you will return"[1]—horizontal smudge. It was a cadence, a buzz that filled the room. They said it over and over, once to each person.

The bowl of ashes at the end of my line was held by a tall, gray-haired man whom I didn't know. He smiled at me in a grandfatherly way. When I stood in front of him, he marked my forehead twice and told me, his face close to mine, that ashes were my starting blocks and my finish line. I went back to my seat, then for a while afterward I was caught up in watching the room. Everywhere I looked—right, left, in front, behind—there were two solemn gray smudges on every face.

It was half a year after everything. My fast was completed. I had kissed a man twice. I had failed tremendously in all kinds of other ways. Grace had been happening to me with such ferocity that I had actually begun to recognize it and even expect it. For decades of life and faith I had taken meticulous care to keep my nose clean—now I was wearing my sin and brokenness on my forehead.

Glancing around the room, I was glad to publicly admit that I'm fallen. I was grateful for the soot-smudged folks who were there with me, showing me how.

Ladder Ways

HERE IS HOW God's grace makes a community. When the gospel happens to a person—when someone understands she doesn't deserve to be forgiven and at the same time she sees that God forgives her, and when someone, in spite of his undeservingness, receives God's generosity—those people are opened up.

Having been accepted—more than accepted, *loved*—by God for exactly who they are, they can be less afraid of being rejected by people, less afraid of knowing and being known. Understanding that Christ became vulnerable for them to the point of death, they allow themselves to be vulnerable too. As recipients of God's grace, they themselves become more gracious, less judgmental toward others.

They learn to accept and relish the truth that no one person is more deserving of God than any other. This shatters walls everywhere.

Before breaking my vow, I had feared that my mistakes would separate me from people. So having broken it, I thought I would do everything in my power to keep the whole story to myself. But after I confessed to Cora that first Tuesday after the wedding, after only half a second's pause on the other side of the line, her voice came to me, light and sweet. "Oh," she said—Cora, with her conservative politics and her cerebral Hebrew studies and her hair in a bun—"everybody kisses everybody at weddings."

Then I heard the pages of her Bible rustling from a couple states away—such a familiar sound on one of our Tuesday phone calls. "If it's okay with you," she told me, "I'd like to read some things."

Cora read from Romans, chapters 3 and 5 and 6 and 8.

"Everyone has sinned; we all fall short of God's glorious standard. Yet God, with undeserved kindness, declares that we are righteous."[1]

"Since we have been made right in God's sight by faith, we have peace with God because of what Jesus Christ our Lord has done for us."[2]

"When we died with Christ we were set free from the power of sin."[3]

"Now there is no condemnation for those who belong to Christ Jesus."[4]

The words washed over me and quieted me. By the time we eventually prayed and hung up, I had learned that Cora was not only a friend; she was my comrade in grace.

After that I got braver. I told several more people about

the post-wedding night with the groomsman. I told my family, I told my close friends, I told the teenagers in the small group I led at church, I told girls I spoke to at the weekend seminars.

Once again, the response was not at all what I would have expected. First of all, people seemed overjoyed to learn I had royally failed my lofty standards. Not that they were vindictive—nobody got on my case or gave me a lecture. And not that they trivialized it—only one person tried to convince me that kissing the groomsman didn't count and that the vow was still intact. And only one person wanted to take me out for a drink to celebrate the end of Saving My First Kiss. Everybody else seemed to understand how easy it can be to break one's word. They seemed glad to add another failed and grateful soul to their ranks.

Shortly after my own confession, other people started coming forward with sinfulness too. Each of two close friends admitted to having slept with a boyfriend, pre-marriage, years earlier. The timing of these disclosures didn't seem coincidental—neither had told me about this until after they learned I had broken my vow. After their confessions, I was surprised to find that I didn't view my two friends any differently than I had before. This was a change; in the past I would've judged hastily and harshly. But I was beginning to understand that in their shoes, I might have made a decision that was every bit as poor and horrendous and stupid, or maybe it would have been worse.

The strata of life were shifting. Suddenly the ladder-faith I had always clung to, an unending climb toward the top, wasn't leading me anywhere. "Follow me," the Good Shepherd says. The call to join his expedition is to follow

226 || CRAVING GRACE

him as part of a pack. All the followers are on even-level ground, equally undeserving, equally able to be astounded by his love.

One of my favorite examples of this: A few years ago, probably just after college, I went to Gram's house over lunch on a summer Saturday. She had prepped a meal and dessert; we ate together and then when the meal was over, Gram went to a kitchen drawer and pulled out her daily Bible devotional, a little booklet called *Today*.

Gram didn't talk about faith with her grandkids much necessarily, but she read from *Today* every day, and whenever we visited for a meal we were sure to read it with her. There was always a Scripture passage, a brief commentary, and a short prayer; Gram would read all three aloud, then after reading the day's page she would simply close the booklet, place it on the table, and ask that everybody pray the Lord's Prayer with her.

I don't remember which passage we read that afternoon a few years ago, but I remember it was about Jesus and his disciples having a conversation, and I remember how it affected Gram. After she finished reading she was quiet for a moment. She didn't close *Today*; instead for a while she studied the still-open pages in her hands. Then she looked up at me.

"He talked with his disciples like that!" she said, and I had never heard her voice so full of joy. It sounded almost overcome.

"He was God and they were people, but he talked with them just like how you would talk with a friend!"

She wiped a tear from her eye. She smiled and sighed a long, awestruck sigh.

Freeloading
Ain't for Sissies

THE CURRENT SUMMER

Out in the pasture and paddocks on the farm, The
Ladies fill their time in two primary ways. They eat and
they sleep, and both activities are done collectively. When
they sleep it's typically in a cluster on the ground: six full-
grown sheep in an area no bigger than ten feet square.
When they eat it's typically in a row: shoulder-to-shoulder
and hip-to-hip. The funniest view of The Ladies at a meal-
time is from the backside, when their six puffy butts and
six triangle tails are practically all you can see.

I was laughing with a friend about The Ladies and their
herd mentality one day when the friend brought up a book
she had recently read. It had been written by a shepherd—in
defense of sheep, she said. Apparently the shepherd-author

makes a case for sheep intelligence, noting that despite their reputation, sheep are smart considering what little they have to work with. They know they're weak and defenseless, so for survival they move by flock. They keep themselves in quantities. This observation was a clear reminder that I have much left to learn as one of Christ's sheep.

What I mean is this: the incredible news of late is that I have fallen in love. Yes, I.

Some months ago I went to visit my brother David and his wife, Christi, in Southern California for a long weekend. At their church's Sunday morning service I was introduced to a tall, handsome Southern California man named Nathan who likes books and hot tea and being hospitable, whose shoulders and intelligence and approachability and jawline make me swoon. Christi invited him to our family lunch that day, and after a meal of animated conversation and strategic seating (he was placed next to only me and across from no one), Nathan proved his astuteness by figuring out that the two of us were being set up. The next afternoon, my last one in town, he invited himself to our family dinner and then suggested a coffee shop we could all go to afterward. Once there, he offered in front of everyone to buy me a drink. I said yes, then savored sips of iced chai between moments of incessant beaming.

The next day, in the time I spent on two quick flights and one short layover, Nathan emailed me twice. That was the start of daily emails to each other, which were upgraded to phone calls and texts only a few weeks later. The time this man and I have known each other has been a whirlwind, but it has been so good it seems to be happening in slow motion.

He sends me flowers. He studies theology for fun. He wakes up at 4 a.m. in California so he can call me as my morning gets started. When I'm sad or confused he listens patiently and gently, waiting as I cry or verbally process or blow my nose repeatedly into the phone. He visited me in Michigan and asked to stay with my parents while he was here. It was important that he get to know them, he said.

I told Nathan about *Saving My First Kiss* and about the Honey Project and about kissing the random grooms-man—yes, even that—something like three weeks in. It was over email; he had asked a question that left me no choice but to bring up the subject. I had been nervous and insecure to share that part of my life with this man whom I found so charming—there was the possibility it would be too much too soon or just an abundance of mess for some-one to deal with. Still, I tried to tell the stories as simply as possible: no disclaimers or apologies, no easy excuses, no making light of what had been serious at the time. It was a long email, and after writing it I was spent.

First thing the next morning, Nathan's response to me included the following:

Thanks for sharing so much of your life, even at the risk of feeling awkward and probably vulnerable. I'm not sure if there's anything I could say or write to make you feel less awkward, but if there is, pretend I just wrote whatever that is. Please pretend that I just wrote that.

Right then and there, I knew I wanted this to be a life-long conversation.

I said to Nathan once, "You make me feel like a gem."

This was in the earliest phases of things, when I was newly love struck and hadn't yet learned how to filter out the worst of my sappiness. It sounded over the top and poorly scripted, like something straight out of a D-list romantic comedy.

Nathan responded without pause and with a smile that can only be called adoring. There wouldn't have been time for him to make even a single comparison to cheesy movie lines. "You," he said, "are the entire gem mine."

Yes, I.

But there is a catch, and it feels like a big one. Here we are, having fallen in love and discussed marriage and started thinking about plans—yet Nathan is an active-duty officer in the Marine Corps. In a couple of weeks he will have to deploy to Iraq for a year. A year. In Iraq. And while I expect I can handle separation and even limited communication, what I'm not sure I can handle is the possibility that he could be hurt, that he might not make it safely home. Iraq is postwar now, Nathan keeps reminding me; the chances of his being hurt there are probably smaller than in most major U.S. cities. Still, I am almost constantly thinking about insurgents and rocket-propelled grenade launchers and IEDs. That's because for me, this fear isn't about chances or likelihoods. I'm not even sure it's about Nathan all that much. Mostly it's about God, and it's about my retaining a taste for his sweetness.

I am trying not to slip back into my old habits of bartering with God for the things I want: *I will be faithful forever if you bring him home and if you let us get married and stay that way for a long while.* I am trying to keep from forgetting that grace is God's ultimate, sweet gift and that it has already been extended. I am trying not to doubt that

God knows what I need and that he gives it—and that sometimes he even gives generously more. But that kind of thing was so easy to disbelieve in the past; it seemed the proof kept pointing in every other direction. Which is probably why at the moment my risk of doubting again is at fever pitch.

I share all this with Marie one Saturday morning in the yard at the farm. I tell her I've been catching myself speculating as to whether or not God has dished out the worst of my romance woes yet. Maybe he put Nathan in my life for these three months to get my hopes up and get me feeling head over heels, only to rip the love out of my life for good. Maybe this is just the setup for the next, hugest disappointment. I tell Marie that I've been letting myself wonder whether that's the kind of character I can count on from God. I tell her that it has gotten so bad I've even been thinking about fasting again to try to keep some perspective. Maybe I'll swear off sweets during the deployment, I tell her, as a way of reminding myself that God has already proved himself sweet.

At this point in our conversation, I'm feeling slightly better because I've been able to share my thoughts with a friend and let off some steam. I'm assuming that's the end of the conversation for now; maybe I'll pray and consider the fasting idea again sometime later, when I'm alone in my car or in my bedroom. At this point I'm definitely leaning away from another fast—six months was difficult enough the first time, and a year without sweets would be crazy long. Besides, I learned the lesson already. Right?

Wrong, as it turns out. Because Marie is thinking like one smart sheep.

"If you decide to go through with the fast, let me know," Marie says. "I'd like to fast for this with you." Before I can even tell her what an unhinged idea that is, Marie is already continuing. "And I'll talk with Kay and Jenny to see if they want to fast too. It would be a cool way to support each other."

Cool, she calls it. Meanwhile, my mind has gone straight to memories of chocolate cravings. From there it goes to gummy candy, which is Jenny's guilty pleasure, and to Kay's daily, beloved twenty ounces of Diet Coke. It goes to all the sacrifices that these people are already making for me every day. So I am seriously doubting whether Marie has any idea what she's talking about. I am expecting that if I let the topic lie for a week or two, nobody else will think about it again.

But the next Sunday evening when we all get together, the idea has exploded. Kay and Jenny have questions about which things are on the Don't Eat list—with Nathan leaving in a matter of weeks, they want to start the process of weaning themselves from sweets soon. Kay says that every time she wants a Diet Coke, she plans to remind herself that God is her true sweetness. Jenny is willing to give up the gummies. Matthew says he'll join our fast every Monday for the deployment year. Kay and Matthew's oldest daughter wants to do Mondays too. Then somebody suggests that we break our fast once a week, that on Sunday evenings when we all meet, we should celebrate this community over sweets. The motion passes heartily. So just like that, it seems there's not much else to be decided. They have committed with me, all of them. A year without sweets. A year of God's sweetness.

This is the kind of sacrifice that makes a community. It's beyond anything I could earn or repay, well beyond my deserving. The only way to respond to such an offer is to reject it entirely or to accept and be humbly grateful. And it is too generous a gift to reject.

So I accept it, all of it. I accept that the love is real and self-giving, that it's possible for me to welcome the free meals here on the farm, not to mention the zero rent and the uneven chore distribution. I accept that I can leave the pots and pans for somebody else to scrub, even though I didn't do any cooking or baking or grocery shopping. I accept that the mail will be gathered and the trash will be taken out, and that I don't have to feel obligated to think about it or do it.

The acceptance is difficult. It requires trusting that comfort will come out of something that feels only abrasive. In this it confounds logic and defies reason. But here is a love made possible because of God's love, which broods over me and which surpasses all knowledge and sense. Here is a grace made possible through Grace. And Grace has a long aftertaste of sweetness, worth every arduous gulp.

Fifty-Two Sundays

THE CURRENT SUMMER

Nathan leaves U.S. soil for Iraq on a Thursday, so it is on Thursday that we all quit sweets. After three full days of fasting, we get together that Sunday evening to share the first of our fifty-two deployment desserts. We have been planning and talking about and looking forward to the dish all week. Digging in, we talk about our horrible cravings and we talk about grace, and it's a start, at least. It is something to feast on.

Acknowledgments

MY THANKS GO out to countless people for their part in helping see this project through to completion; there's no telling how even a first draft could've happened without them. I'm glad to acknowledge in particular the following set of folks, who have demonstrated much grace toward me and for whom I am deeply grateful.

Skilled agent Greg Johnson and the whole team at WordServe Literary Agency—I cannot express how much bolstering your partnership provides.

The fine staff at Tyndale House Publishers, especially the editorial team of Sarah Atkinson, Jan Long Harris, and Stephanie Voiland, all of whom proved their excellence again and again; Sharon Leavitt, for constant encouragement and support; Sarah Drake, who came up with the title everybody had been trying to think of; Julie Chen and team for the cover—I revised after seeing it, in hopes that the writing would live up to the design; and the collective creative genius of the marketing and sales team, led by Nancy Clausen and Yolanda Sidney.

Those teachers, artists, and scholars who were repeatedly instrumental in shaping the content of this book (not to mention me) as I wrote it: Rob Bell, Frederick Buechner, Steve DeNeff, Ed Dobson, Sara Groves, Shane Hipps, Timothy Keller, Matt Krick, Matt Laidlaw, Brad Nelson, Nichole Nordeman, Don Sampson, Bill Stephens, and Ray Vander Laan.

Mars Hill Bible Church in Grandville, Michigan, which helps show me what it is to be a people changed by grace.

Courtney, who put up with all kinds of roommate conversations about writing and men, and who could always make me laugh and feel encouraged.

Ray for the honey bear story, the video series that includes "The Lord Is My Shepherd," and so much more.

The Thomason Park Fellowship in Quantico for great discussions and instant friendships. Special thanks to Shawn Campbell and Mike Vincent, whose comments helped me realize that my sheep metaphor could carry more weight.

Dr. Mary Brown, who taught me to "go with the vehicle" and whose lessons are still running through my head when I write.

The incredible staff, volunteers, and high school students of Anthem. This includes Kirk Eklund, who often specified that he should be mentioned by name.

My friends and former coworkers on both the Winning At Home and Mars Hill staffs, especially those who read early drafts: Brad, Lori, and Steve; and the Communications Team, which became family to me: Beth, Jenn, Laurie, Lee, Michelle, and Mike.

Friends who generously shared with me their rooms,

meals, and coffee supplies, and who offered up faithful prayers while I was writing: the Davises, the Ertmans, the Facklers, the Lades, the Mulders, the Neikirks, the Overbeeks, the Reeds, the Riojases (as I write this, I sit cozily on the Riojas' futon), the Stepps, the VanderKloks, the VanDykes, and the VerWyses.

Hilarious and unflinching girlfriends, mentors, and fellow d-group members who always asked how the book was going: Andrea, Annie, Annie (yes, there are two Annies), Beth, Brynne, Christina, Doni, Emilie, Jenna, Jettie, Julia, Linda, Linda (two Lindas, too), Nicole, Rachel, and Sarah.

My parents, siblings, and in-laws, all of whom make me laugh like crazy and help make me better than I am: Ben and Faye; Noah and Paige; Sarah, David, and Christiana; and Robert, Shirley, and Evangeline.

Nathan, who is the collaborator and encourager I never dared ask for, beyond my best thoughts and boldest prayers. To me he is the surprise hero of not just this book but the first one too.

God has been gracious and good, and continually, surprisingly sweet.

Notes

FEELING UNLED
1. Psalm 91:4
2. From Ephesians 3:17-19, ESV

FAITH PLAYING FAIR
1. Job 1:1, NLT
2. Job 19:25
3. Job 31:6
4. Job 38:2-4, 34-35; Job 39:26-27; Job 40:2, NLT
5. Job 42:3, 5-6, NLT

GREENLESSNESS
1. Psalm 23:1-2, NKJV
2. Supplemental information was found at "Green Pastures," That the World May Know, http://www.followtherabbi.com/Brix?pageID=1573.

RUDE, NUDE
1. "Nakedness and the Holiness of God," given by Timothy J. Keller on 3/21/93, accessed by MP3. Copyright by Redeemer Presbyterian Church, New York, NY.

NOT TESTING THE LORD
1. Matthew 4:7, NLT

ONLY BROTHERLY
1. Matthew 26:33, NLT
2. Matthew 26:75, NLT

3. John 21:15-17, NLT
4. Matthew 26:33, NLT
5. John 10:11, NLT
6. John 21:19, NLT

SEXY, CURSING, DRINKING PHASE

1. Erika Bullmann Flores, translated from Dr. Martin Luther's *Saemmtliche Schriften*, Dr. Johann Georg Walch, editor (St. Louis: Concordia Publishing House), vol. 15, col. 2585-2590. The full quote reads: "If the mercy is true, you must therefore bear the true, not an imaginary sin. God does not save those who are only imaginary sinners. Be a sinner, and let your sins be strong [sin boldly], but let your trust in Christ be stronger, and rejoice in Christ who is the victor over sin, death, and the world."

TO ASHES

1. See Genesis 3:19.

LADDER WAYS

1. Romans 3:23-24, NLT
2. Romans 5:1, NLT
3. Romans 6:7, NLT
4. Romans 8:1, NLT

About the Author

Lisa Velthouse is a freelance writer and speaker who has been working in communications and ministry for more than a decade. She got her start in publishing at the age of seventeen, when she was selected from more than one thousand applicants to write a year's worth of columns for *Brio* magazine. While writing for *Brio*, Lisa began speaking at national evangelical events for teens, and she also came up with the idea for her first book, *Saving My First Kiss*, which was published shortly after she turned twenty-one. In the years that followed, she worked as a ghostwriter and then served for two years on staff at Mars Hill Bible Church in Grandville, Michigan.

Lisa's writing has been noted in *Publishers Weekly* and Focus on the Family publications, and she has been a guest on numerous nationwide radio and television programs. Her speaking tours have taken her across the United States and abroad. She is married to Nathan, an officer in the U.S. Marine Corps; they live wherever military assignments take them. Read more from Lisa at lisavelthouse.com.

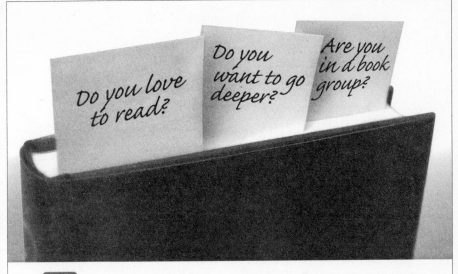

REVELATIONS
of a
Single Woman

loving the life i didn't expect

CONNALLY GILLIAM

Turning our culture's *Sex and the City* worldview upside down, Connally Gilliam shows you how to celebrate God's enticing, life-giving promises, even when life takes you down a path you didn't plan for.

"Matt Mikalatos's imagination is, simply put, miraculous. I loved this book."
—A.J. JACOBS, *New York Times* bestselling author of *A Year of Living Biblically*

Imaginary Jesus

A not-quite-true story...

MATT MIKALATOS

CP0458